the *SOUL* of a BUTTERFLY

Reflections on Life's Journey

Muhammad Ali
with Hana Yasmeen Ali

Photographs by
Howard Bingham

Simon & Schuster
New York   London   Toronto   Sydney

SIMON & SCHUSTER
Rockefeller Center
1230 Avenue of the Americas
New York, NY 10020

For information about special discounts for bulk purchases,
please contact Simon & Schuster Special Sales:
1-800-456-6798 or business@simonandschuster.com

Designed by Julian Peploe

Portions of *The Soul of a Butterfly* draw on previously published material from
Muhammad Ali: His Life and Times by Thomas Hauser, © 1991 by Thomas Hauser
and Muhammad Ali, published by Simon & Schuster, used by permission.

Manufactured in the United States of America

10 9 8 7 6 5 4 3 2 1

Library of Congress Control Number: 2004045345

ISBN 0-7432-5569-0

To my parents Odessa and Cassius Clay, with love
—Muhammad Ali

To my Guardian Angels. They know who they are.
—Hana Yasmeen Ali

With my third wife, Veronica, and our daughters, Hana and Laila.

contents

Love is a net where hearts
are caught like fish.
—*Sufi Wisdom*

a LETTER *to* | THE WORLD

Myths are about gods, legends are about heroes, and fairy tales describe the endless worlds of magic and dreams. This book is neither myth nor fairy tale, but the story of a legend with unwavering conviction. In the following pages you will read about a man who asked his heart what actions to take, and his heart replied like the beat of a drum that has yet to fade. You will read about a man who stood up for those who could not stand up for themselves. About a man who stared adversity in the face. A man who shared himself with the world and all who came his way.

You will read about a man who embodies the conflicts, struggles, and hopes of hundreds of years, a man who mesmerized the world with his artistry in the boxing ring, and won its respect with his courage outside it. Yet, his greatest accomplishments—love, kindness, and generosity—all occurred outside the spotlight. Throughout his life, he has moved us to tears, of both joy and sorrow. He has found a home in the heart of the people of all nations, and become the epitome of a champion and a hero.

It is said that more has been written about Muhammad Ali than any other living person. When you have a heart as big as the world, the world wants to write about it. The difference between this book and all the others about him is that this book is from his heart.

In the following pages, you will see the world through my father's eyes. You will learn about his dreams, his obstacles, his heartbreaks, and his victories from his youth to the present moment. This book is a journey through the defining moments in my father's life. It is filled with his personal recollections, occasionally sprinkled with my own memories, and laced with the stories and poems that touched his heart.

I have witnessed the humanity and compassion of this man whose innocence of heart has gone untouched by time, a man with the soul of a butterfly. It has been a gift and an honor working with my father to help share his thoughts, beliefs, and motivations with the world. If we all have parts to play in life, this is the story of the man who played the part of love.

Daddy, you are my constant truth, my strength, my heaven on earth. Thank you for being there for me, thank you for believing in me, thank you for holding my hand in the dark and always standing by me. You have been more than just my father; you have been my teacher of love, my friend, and my guardian angel. I cherish you and adore you more than you could ever know. God bless you, Daddy. You are my inspiration.

with love,
hana yasmeen ali

You will never truly know
the depth of my father's soul,
how deep his dignity flows.
To love and give is all he's known,
And his honor is a virtue of its own.
Words are not enough to tell his story.
Colors aren't lovely enough to depict his face.
Legend is not sturdy enough to uphold his name.
His spirit has surpassed our descriptive plane.
A billion stars could never replace,
The space his heart has filled.
A universe of doubt could never erase,
The faith his heart has embraced.
No picture has ever sufficiently captured
The smile in his angelic eyes,
And no book will ever fully explain
the beauty that Ali has defined.

—HANA YASMEEN ALI

Ali

INTRODUCTION

People were always asking me what I was going to do after I retired from boxing. My response then was as it is now: During my boxing career, you did not see the real Muhammad Ali. You just saw a little boxing and a little show-manship. It was after I retired from boxing that my true work began. I had more time then to develop my spiritual being the way that I once developed my muscles and agility.

When I look at the world, I see that many people build big beautiful houses but live in broken homes. We spend more time learning how to make a living than we do learning to make a life. What I hope to share with you are the beliefs that I have come to live by. Many of the philosophies, stories, and ideals that have touched my soul and inspired my heart I learned from my study of Islam. I have shared this knowledge with my family and friends; now I offer it to the world.

Over the years my religion has changed and my spirituality has evolved. Religion and spirituality are very different, but people often confuse the two. Some things cannot be taught, but they can be awakened in the heart. Spirituality is recognizing the divine light that is within us all. It doesn't belong to any particular religion; it belongs to everyone.

People have asked me if I still work on my faith. The truth is, I can talk all day about my faith because more than anything else in my life, I believe in God. If all of the oceans on Earth were ink, and all of the trees were pens, they still would not be sufficient to write down the knowledge God has. Knowing that God has power like that keeps me humble. The more I study about God and Islam, the more I realize how little I know. So, I am still studying, and I'm still learning because there's nothing as great as working for God.

Truly great people in history never wanted to be great for themselves. All they wanted was the chance to do good for others and be close to God. I'm not perfect. I know that I still have things to work out, and I'm working on them. There are certain things I have done that I am not proud of, especially when they caused pain to others. I ask God for forgiveness.

No matter where I go, everybody recognizes my face and knows my name. People love and admire me; they look up to me. That's a lot of power and influence for one man to have, so I know I have a responsibility to use my fame the right way. That's one of the reasons I've always tried to be good to everyone no matter their color, religion, or position in life. Though some people may see themselves as better or more important than others, in God's eyes we are all equal, and it's what is in our hearts that matters.

People say that I gave away too much money during my boxing career.

They write about how some people took advantage of me, stole from me, and how I let them get away with it. Even when I knew people were cheating me, what was important was how I behaved, because I have to answer to God. I can't be responsible for other people's actions: They will have to answer to God themselves. Throughout my life, I never sought retribution against those who hurt me because I believe in forgiveness. I have practiced forgiving, just as I want to be forgiven. Only God knows what's in a person's heart, his true intentions. He sees and hears all things.

Many people around me had their hands out, and I tried to help as many of them as I could. There's nothing wrong with that. I gave to people in need, even when I could have used the money myself, because God had made me rich enough. Now, as I look back, it seems that the more I gave in the name of God, the more he has given back to me. I try not to speak about the charities and people I help, because I believe we can only be truly generous when we expect nothing in return.

At night when I go to bed, I ask myself, "If I don't wake up tomorrow, would I be proud of how I lived today." With that question in mind, I have tried to do as many good deeds as I can, whether it is standing up for my faith, signing an autograph, or simply shaking a person's hand. I'm just trying to make people happy and get into heaven.

My concept of religion has broadened over the years. My mother was a Baptist, and my father was a Methodist. They both believed that Jesus was the son of God. I don't believe that, but I believe he was an important prophet like Moses. I believe that on judgment day, my parents will be in heaven, not because they were without fault, but because they were decent, loving human beings, and they believed in God. We all have the same God, we just serve him differently. Rivers, lakes, ponds, streams, oceans, all have different names, but they all contain water. So do religions have different names, and they all contain truth, expressed in different ways, forms, and times. It doesn't matter whether you're a Muslim, a Christian, or a Jew. When you believe in God, you should believe that all people are part of one family. If you love God, you can't love only some of his children.

This book is a reflection of my life, it describes some of my most memorable experiences, and tells the story of how I came to be the man I am today. I have come a long way since I started boxing. I've traveled all around the world and met all types of people. I believe that God beautified the planet by spreading everyone out and making us different. The goal of our nations should be to work on understanding, respecting our differences, and celebrating our similarities. We should appreciate the beauty in the diversity. It would be a boring world, if every flower were the same shape, color, and size.

One of the most important aspects of my spirituality has been gradually recognizing all of the moments in my life when God was working through me, inside and outside the ring. Growing up, I had trouble reading and spelling. I barely graduated from high school. They have a name for what I have, *dyslexia*. But back when I was in school, teachers figured that kids with learning difficulties were stupid. School was challenging for me, but I found a way to work it out. When I came to a brick wall, I didn't give up and quit; I found my way around, under, or over it. I found a way to work with what God gave me. When I read or hear something that I think is valuable, something that speaks to me of the world as I feel it, I focus on those parts. I memorize them. When something seems true to me, it becomes part of me. That is how I learn.

I felt God was always working through me. He filled me with wisdom, confidence, self-assurance, and awareness. I studied life and I studied people. I may be poor at reading and writing, but when it comes to love, compassion, and other feelings of the heart, I am rich. There is an old saying that I've recited over the years. It goes like this: "Where is man's wealth? His wealth is in his knowledge. If his wealth is in the bank, he doesn't possess it." My wealth is in my knowledge of self, love, and spirituality. I've tried to use my knowledge to be a good representative of my people. I can't be blind, because if the blind lead the blind they all fall into a ditch.

My soul has grown over the years, and some of my views have changed. As long as I'm alive, I will continue to try to understand more because the work of the heart is never done. All through my life I have been tested. My will has been tested, my courage has been tested, my strength has been tested. Now my patience and endurance are being tested. Every step of the way I believe that God has been with me. And, more than ever, I know that he is with me now. I have learned to live my life one step, one breath, and one moment at a time, but it was a long road. I set out on a journey of love, seeking truth, peace, and understanding. I am still learning.

GOD BLESS
the world

I hope that one day all
nations great and small
will be able to stand up and say
we lived in pursuit of peace for all.

Maybe then there will come a day
when instead of saying, "God bless America,"
or "God bless some other country,"
everyone everywhere will say,
"God bless the world."

competition *for* LOVE

*Love is the only thing that every soul
brings to earth with it.*

A Hindu poet said: "The desire to love brought me to earth, and the same desire to see the beloved I am taking with me to heaven."

Wouldn't it be a beautiful world if just 10 percent of the people who believe in the power of love would compete with one another to see who could do the most good for the most people? So many of us enjoy taking part in competitions, why not hold a competition of love instead of one that leads to jealousy and envy? If we continue to think and live as if we belong only to different cultures and different religions, with separate missions and goals, we will always be in self-defeating competition with each other.

*   *   *

Once we realize we are all members of humanity, we will want to compete in the spirit of love.

In a competition of love we would not be running against one another, but with one another. We would be trying to gain victory for all humanity. If I am a faster runner than you, you may feel bad seeing me pass you in the race, but if you know that we are both racing to make our world better, you will feel good knowing that we are all racing toward a common goal, a mutual reward.

In a competition of love we'll all share in the victory, no matter who comes in first.

A heart enlightened by love is more precious than all of the diamonds and gold in the world.

inspired by *a sufi message*

*The outer beauty of a
person must merge
with the inner beauty
and become one.
This is the source
of true beauty.*

—Sufi Wisdom

L O V E

THE IDEAL OF BEAUTY

True beauty is found in the heart of the beholder.

As I begin the story of my journey, I would like to share a short story that I learned from the teachings of Sufism. There once was a king who enjoyed spending his spare time in the company of philosophers and friends, debating various subjects. One afternoon, the debate concerned where beauty lies. As they were talking together on the terrace of the palace, the king and his friends could see their children playing in the courtyard. The king called to one of his servants. He gave him a jeweled crown and asked him to place it upon the head of the most beautiful child in the courtyard.

The servant took the crown and walked out to the middle of the courtyard, where all the children were playing as their parents watched from the terrace.

First the servant placed the crown on the head of the king's son. He saw that it suited him well. The boy was a handsome lad but, somehow, the servant was not satisfied. He tried it on the head of another child, and another, until he came upon his own son, who was sitting in the corner. He placed the jeweled crown on his son's head and found that it suited him wonderfully.

The servant then took his son by the hand and led him to the king. When he reached the terrace, he bowed his head and spoke. "Sire, I have found that of all the children, the crown suits this one best. Indeed, if I tell the truth I must say this. I am ashamed to appear so bold, for the child is the son of my humble self."

Then the king and those beside him laughed very heartily and thanked the servant, for they all thought his son to be very ugly indeed. The king walked over to the servant and said, "You have certainly told me what I wish to know: It is the heart that perceives beauty."

THE EARLY YEARS

With my brother, Rahaman, and my parents, Mama Bird and Papa Cash, soon after I became an Olympic champion.

the FOUNDATION of | *LIFE*

I can remember, when I was just a kid in Louisville, Kentucky, my mother would wake my brother and me early every Sunday morning. She would come into our room, kiss us on the forehead, and say in a gentle whisper, "Wake up, tinky baby, wake up, Rudy, we're going to thank the Lord!"

My mother would sometimes call me "GG," too, because those were the first syllables I had spoken. After I won the Gold Gloves, I told her that from the very beginning I was trying to say "Golden Gloves." I thought my mother had a tiny little bird nose. I don't know why I thought that, because birds don't have noses, but from the moment I said it we all started calling her Mama Bird. After waking me and Rudy, Bird would cook us a nice breakfast. While we ate, she would iron our best clothes and lay them out on the bed. Then she would call us for a bath. After getting dressed, Rudy and I would go outside to sit on the front porch and shoot marbles before we headed off for Sunday school.

I can remember trying hard not to get dirty. I knew I looked handsome in my freshly ironed shirt and bow tie. When Bird walked out beside my father, Cassius Clay, or Cash, I remember looking up at them with pride, thinking how pretty she looked and how handsome he was with his thick black mustache. Cash would often say to me, "Most men envy me because they can't grow a mustache as long and thick as mine."

What he said has always stuck with me. I think that to him, his mustache was a source of pride. To this day, every so often, I let my own grow.

I had a strong foundation growing up; my parents were loving, affectionate people. Ever since I can remember, my father was always hugging and kissing us. He would say "give me those jaws" (his term for kissing our cheeks). Then he kissed us until our cheeks turned red. Cash always made me feel important. Although, at times my father had a quick temper, and my parents had disagreements, I had a happy home life and I knew that I was loved. My parents made me feel special. When it wasn't my father's affection, it was my mother's stories. Mama Bird was always telling me about the time I was born. She said that I was such a pretty baby, everyone thought I was a girl, and that from the moment they brought me home, Cash was "biting my jaws." My parents weren't perfect, but they each had a loving nature. My father was a painter. He made his living painting murals and signs. Almost every Baptist church around Louisville has his work in them. My father was very talented; I have one of his paintings hanging on my office wall, right above my desk. Cash used to tell people that he wasn't just a painter; he was an artist. Sometimes he would take me and Rudy to work with him. Cash would teach us how to mix the paint and lay out a sign. I could draw a little, but nothing special. It was Rudy that took after Cash. He is an artist, too. Cash used to say that if it weren't for the way things were then, a lot more people would have known what he could do. My father raised us well. He made sure we were surrounded by good people, taught us to always confront the things we feared, and to try to be the best at whatever we did. After delivering his advice, Cash would say, "These are the things my father said to me, and you don't learn them by accident, they have to be taught."

Cash was one of a kind; he was full of life and energy. He loved hugging, kissing, talking, and debating. He was my father and my friend. He was at my side when he could be and we had a lot more good times together than bad.

Sometimes, after school, when we finished our homework, Rudy and I would play outside with some of the other kids in the neighborhood. I used to ask Rudy to throw rocks at me to see if he could hit me. He thought that I was crazy, but no matter how many he threw, he could never hit me. I was too fast. I was running left, and right, ducking, dodging, and jumping out of the way. My brother and I had a lot of fun together, we never really got into fights. My mother used to tell me that when I was about four, whenever she would try to discipline Rudy, I would step in and say, "Don't you spank my baby." Rudy and I have always been close. He's my younger brother and I love him.

I wasn't much trouble as a child, but when I did cut up, Mama Bird just sat me in a corner and put an old bear head rug in the middle of the floor. I was so scared of it, I didn't move an inch. I thought the rug might jump up and bite me. My mother was a gentle lady. She always spoke in a tender voice and I never heard her say a bad thing about anyone. She didn't gossip or meddle in other people's business. She taught us that prejudice was wrong, and to always treat people with love and respect. My mother loved to cook, eat, make clothes, and be with her family. I loved her very much; there's never been anyone better to me in my whole life.

I learned a lot from my parents while I was growing up. I noticed how they remained dignified in the face of injustice. I saw how they responded to the people around them; I witnessed how my mother would forgive, not hate. And how Cash always held his head high and he worked hard. Growing up, we were poor in terms of money, but we were rich to have had so much love and pride in our household. We were raised with strong values and learned the importance of integrity and compassion. More important than the words, I learned by their example.

My mother was a Baptist and my father was a Methodist, but we always went to my mother's church. She taught us everything she believed was true about God. Cash used to say that he let Mama Bird raise us her way, because she was a good Baptist, and that a woman is better than a man, so we should follow our mother.

When I was in junior high school I applied for a job cleaning the blackboards and desks and doing odd jobs at Spalding College in Louisville. Sister James Ella gave me the job. I made a few dollars a week, working under the direction of Sister Ann. Sister James Ella was a sweet lady. She showed me how to clean shelves and sweep the floor. She passed away a few years ago, but I will always remember her. I had a good childhood. There were obstacles, and hardships, but I remained on the straight path. I kept my values in mind, and my faith remained strong. Although my religion would change later in my life, God was always in my heart.

My mother once told me that my confidence in myself made her believe in me. I thought that was funny, because it was her confidence in me that strengthened my belief in myself. I didn't realize it then, but from the very beginning, my parents were helping me build the foundation for my life.

*Think well of
all, be patient
with all, and try
to find the
good in all.*

the

INNOCENCE

of youth

When my youngest child, Asaad, was about four years old, he said something that brought tears to my eyes. My daughters Hana and Laila walked into the hotel room where my wife, Lonnie, and I were staying in Los Angeles; Asaad was playing with his mother on the bed. It was summer, and Asaad had been swimming all week, so his skin had gotten darker. When Laila walked into the room and saw him, she picked him up and gave him a big hug and kiss. She then innocently said, "Wow, Asaad, you sure got black today!"

Asaad replied, "I'm not black, I'm clean!"

What he said made me think about when I was his age, and how different the world was then. Asaad was still new to the world. He hadn't yet learned about the concept of color. His mind and heart were still innocent. And I thought to myself how wonderful it would be if we could all hold on to the innocence of youth.

*   *   *

Holding onto my innocence as I grew up in the 1950s and 1960s was difficult. I began to recognize the injustice of segregation around me. There were restaurants with signs that read, "Whites Only" and "No Coloreds Allowed." Blacks could only drink from water fountains and use restrooms that were labeled "Colored." My brother and I didn't run into any real trouble with the white kids, but there were times when we were called "nigger" and asked to leave certain neighborhoods. We didn't experience the same violence that many blacks did in other parts of the South, but Louisville was segregated. It was strange going out into a world that looked at blacks as second-class citizens while being raised with pride and self-awareness at home. Although my parents tried their best to shield us from the cruelties of the world, some problems were inevitable.

One of my first encounters with prejudice happened when I was too young to remember, but I've heard my mother tell the story. She and I were standing at a bus stop. It was a hot day and I was thirsty, so we walked up the block to a small diner, where she asked if she could have a cup of water for her son. The man said he could not help us and closed the door in our faces. I can only imagine the pain my mother felt when she tried to find the words to explain why the man would not give me a glass of water. Even during these times my mother would say, "Hating is wrong, no matter who does the hating. It's just plain wrong."

When I was a little older, I saw a newspaper with a front-page story about a boy named Emmett Till. He was a black boy about the same age as me, who was brutalized and lynched while on vacation in Mississippi, supposedly for whistling at a white woman. A picture of him in his coffin was in the newspapers, with a gruesome description of what had been done to him. It made me sick, and it scared me. I was full of sadness and confusion. I didn't realize how hateful some people could be until that day.

Although I didn't know Emmett Till personally, from that day on I could see him in every black boy and girl. I imagined him playing and laughing. As I looked at his picture in the paper, I realized that this could just as easily have been a story about me or my brother. They caught the people that did it and put them on trial, but an all-white jury found the defendants not guilty—even though there had been eyewitness testimony that the defendants had been the ones who had kidnapped the boy. Emmett's mother said, "When something like that happened to the Negroes in the south, I said, 'That's their business, not mine.' Now I know how wrong I was. The murder of my son has shown me that what happens to any of us anywhere in the world had better be the business of us all." I believe that this is true.

I knew that my heart could harden in a world with so much pain, confusion, and injustice. Somehow, I knew that if I were going to survive, I could not become bitter. I would have to love even those who could not give it in return. I would have to learn to forgive even those who would not—or my soul would wither away.

BLACK
Is
Beautiful

When I looked in the mirror I was proud of what I saw, but there were many Black people who didn't want to be Black anymore. Little Black boys and girls had no public role models. We didn't have any heroes who looked like us. There was no one for us to identify with, and we didn't know where we fit in. Even pictures of Jesus Christ were always White. I was taught that Jesus was the son of God, and I wondered if God looked like Jesus, too. Jesus was always depicted with long blond hair and blue eyes. Then I noticed how all of the angels in pictures were White. There were never any pictures of Black angels. And everyone at the Last Supper was White. So, one day, I asked my mother, "What happens to us when we die? Do we go to heaven?"

"Naturally, we go to heaven," she said.

And I said, "Then, what happened to all the Black angels when they took the pictures? Oh, I know. If the White folks go to heaven, the Black angels would be in the kitchen preparing the milk and honey."

That was okay because I didn't like milk and honey anyway. I just wanted some answers. I wanted to know why everything good was always shown as White.

One Halloween, a little Black girl was trick-or-treating around the neighborhood, dressed up in a superhero costume, but her face was painted white. When I asked her why, she said that her sister told her that there was no such thing as a Black superhero. She was right. When I turned on the television, everyone was always White. Superman was White, Santa Claus was White. They even made Tarzan, king of the jungle in Africa, a White man. I noticed that Miss America was always White, and the president living in the White House was White, too. Nothing good reflected our image. At that early age, I could see that something was very wrong. I didn't understand it. I thought that my skin was beautiful, I was proud of the color of my complexion. But everything black was considered bad, and undesirable. Like black cats bring bad luck. Devils' food cake was the dark cake, and angel food cake was the white cake. These may have been subtle messages, but the affects were profound. Every day these messages shaped the images that I and other nonwhite children had of ourselves. I didn't know how, but I knew that I was going to help my people. Somehow, I was going to make a difference in the world. The more injustice that I saw, the stronger my feelings grew. It made me feel that I was here for a reason.

the *purpose* of LIFE

Everything that God created has a purpose. The sun has a purpose. The clouds have a purpose. Rain has a purpose. Trees have a purpose. Animals have a purpose; even the smallest insects, and fish in the sea have a purpose.

Regardless of how large or small, we were all born to accomplish a certain task. It is the knowledge of that purpose that enables every soul to fulfill itself. One person with knowledge of his life's purpose is more powerful than ten thousand working without that knowledge.

It is important for each of us to figure out why we were put here on earth by God. The importance of life is to accomplish the task we were given. Without working on this task, life is meaningless. Human beings have a basic need and desire to accomplish something before they die—to make a difference. When working toward this goal, man has hope and energy. Therefore, it is essential that each of us learn what we were meant to do as early as possible in order to have a satisfying and productive life.

Your purpose may be bigger than mine or another person's, but that doesn't make mine any less important. God would not place a burden on a man's shoulders knowing he could not carry it, nor would he give a person a purpose without significance.

Everyone has his or her own lessons to learn and obstacles to overcome. The experiences should not be weighed against each other because they are all equally important in the end. Each time I thought I had achieved my life's purpose, I discovered it was only another step in my journey. I thought boxing would help me be that public Black role model who was missing while I was growing up. I thought my purpose was to be that hero who showed children that Black is beautiful. I thought my purpose was to be that champion who showed White people they couldn't treat Blacks like second-class citizens. I learned that all of these accomplishments were important, but even more important, I gained a platform that allowed me to carry out my real mission, which has been to encourage all people to respect each other and to live in peace. I am still discovering God's purpose for me.

AWARENESS

I have always had a curious mind. Even as a young child I would think and wonder about things that most kids my age paid no attention to. From the very beginning I was different; I even had chicken pox and measles at the same time. My mother would say that my mind was like the March wind, blowing every which way. I would look into the heavens and wonder about the Creator of all these things. As I grew older, I began to think more about the relationship between man and God. Some of my questions about this relationship were answered, but some of the answers only produced more questions.

I felt I was here to do great things. I felt I had a special place in the world. Something in my heart made me believe it. As the years passed, the feeling grew stronger. When I was about nine years old, I would wake up in the middle of the night and go outside to wait for an angel or a revelation from God. I would sit on the front porch, look up at the stars and wait for a message. I never heard anything, but I never lost faith, because the feeling was so strong in my heart. I didn't know it then, but in the years to come something would happen to put me on the path to discovering my life's purpose. It would take me forward in my journey.

birth of a

DREAM

I discovered my way at the age of twelve.
   Lance Armstrong, a champion himself,
       recently wrote a book called
       It's Not About the Bike.
Well, for me it was all about the bike.

It was the winter of 1954; I just received my red-and-white Schwinn bike for Christmas. A friend and I rode our bikes over to the Louisville Home Show at Columbia Auditorium. There was an annual Black bazaar going on, and we spent the day picking up free samples of food, popcorn, and candy. When it was time to go home, I discovered my bike was gone.

I was so upset I went looking for the police to report it. Someone directed me down to the gym run by a local policeman named Joe Martin, who was teaching young boys to box in his spare time. I told Mr. Martin that I was gonna whup whoever stole my bike. I was half crying and probably didn't look too convincing. I remember Mr. Martin telling me, "Well, you better learn how to fight before you start challenging people that you're gonna whup."

I joined Mr. Martin's gym and began boxing with a vengeance. All of my spare time was spent on training; I was the first one in the gym, and the last to leave. Boxing kept me out of trouble. I trained six days a week and never drank or smoked cigarettes.

Joe Martin was the man who started me out in boxing, but regularly I trained with a Black man named Fred Stoner, who taught me how to jab. If I ever found out who took my bike, I was going to be ready. Mr. Martin produced a local television show called *Tomorrow's Champions* as part of the Columbia Gym's amateur program. It offered instant local celebrity status to his boxers. When I first started boxing, all I wanted was to someday buy my parents a house and own a nice big car. I figured if I could turn pro and get on Saturday night fights, I could make four thousand dollars just for one night. Then my dreams started to grow. When I was in school, sometimes I would pretend that they were announcing my name over the loudspeaker system, saying "Cassius Clay, heavyweight champion of the world." Other times I would draw a picture of a jacket on a piece of paper, and on the back of the jacket I would write, "Cassius Clay, Golden Gloves Winner," or "Cassius Clay, World Heavyweight Champ."

From the beginning, I was determined to be the best boxer. I knew that meant I was going to have to stay focused and work hard. I can remember one occasion when I was in the gymnasium sparring with another kid, named Willy Moran. Willy was a hard hitter who later turned pro. Anyway, I had just finished talking to Mr. Martin about wanting to get a scooter. When I got into the ring, I was still thinking about what color it was going to be. I thought red would be nice. Then, all of a sudden, Boom! I blacked out. I had been knocked out cold. When I woke up, the first thing I said was, "Which way was the scooter going when it hit me?"

That's when I learned the importance of remaining focused. Soon thereafter, I had my first amateur fight. I was twelve years old and weighed about ninety pounds. I can remember walking down the aisle with my father, headed for the ring. When I looked up to see who I was fighting, my eyes widened. It was another beginner named Ronnie O'Keefe. He was a White boy who was a little bigger and a little older than I was. I was scared to death. I looked up at my dad and said, "Cash, do you see who I'm fighting?"

Cash looked me in the eye. "Yes, and we're going to whup him." Hearing my father say that inspired me. Suddenly I felt good, I had my dad in my corner and I won my first fight.

*　　*　　*

At that early age I learned another important lesson. Although I was the one in the ring, I won as part of a team. I continued fighting and training hard. By the time I was eighteen, I had already fought 108 amateur bouts. I won six Kentucky Golden Gloves Championships, two National Golden Gloves tournaments, and two National AAU titles.

It all started coming together, when I realized that boxing was how I was going to succeed in life. People began recognizing that I had a talent, but to the world outside of Louisville, Kentucky, I was still unknown. Before I could change that, there were two more obstacles that I had to overcome. The first was Corky Baker.

the KING *of the* STREET

The first time I saw Corky Baker he was holding one of the football players from my school's team upside down, shaking all the money from his pockets. Corky was short, stocky, and bowlegged; had big muscles and a mean stare; and was older than me. Corky beat up everybody and terrorized the whole neighborhood, including me. He was as mean as he was strong, and had a reputation for knocking out grown men. Corky made money betting on how high he could lift the ends of automobiles.

I always walked around Mr. Martin's Gym and my school confident and proud, except when I heard Corky was on the streets.

Like everybody else, I had to find another way around Corky's block, unless I wanted to pay the toll he charged for the privilege of walking past him. Corky was the undisputed "King of the Streets." In almost every run-in I had with him, I lost. It was really starting to shake me up. Even with all my training and my boxing skills, I knew I would never go far in boxing unless I stopped dodging Corky Baker. He held the crown that would make me feel most confident as a fighter. I thought that if I could whup Corky, I could whup the whole world.

I started talking about how I would whup Corky if I got him in the ring. When Corky found out what I was going around saying, he came looking for me. He said that when he got his hands on me, he was going to tear me apart. My friends Willy and Ronnie and some other neighborhood kids were there when I confronted him. Corky wanted to fight me right then and there, but I knew it would be suicide to fight him in the streets without any rules or regulations and no referee.

So I challenged Corky to a boxing match at Columbia Gym on "Tomorrow's Champions." Corky laughed and said that boxing was for sissies, that it wasn't real fighting. But when everybody started laughing at him and calling him a coward, Corky quickly changed his mind and accepted.

the
SHOWDOWN

When the day of the fight arrived I was scared to death, but I had my father and my brother with me. All my friends from the neighborhood and classmates from Central High were there. It was time for the showdown. Corky and I were about to fight three rounds for the title that would mean the most to me. Whoever won this fight would be the "King of the Street." This wasn't about a financial victory, it was more important than money. I couldn't see myself as a real champion until I stood up to Corky. Now the moment was here, and as I stood in my corner of the ring. I hoped that Corky wouldn't notice that my knees were shaking.

When the bell rang for the first round, I came out moving, throwing jabs, then tried to stay out of his reach.

Corky came out swinging. He was throwing big hard punches that weren't landing. I kept moving, because if Corky hit me, he would have knocked me out. But Corky was quickly becoming tired.

When the bell rang for the second round, Corky came out chasing me, but he couldn't catch me. I was ducking his punches, and I was faster and smarter than he was.

Before the second round was over he said, "This ain't fair" and ran out of the ring and left the gym. I had won the respect of my peers and the title. I had blackened his eye and bloodied his nose. More important, I had faced my fear and gained the self-respect and self-confidence I needed to continue my boxing career.

THE VICTORY
and
THE LESSON

I was now the King of the Street. All my friends and kids from the neighborhood were jumping up and down, shouting,

"We're free, we're free, long live the King, we're free!"

That's when I realized that I didn't just fight Corky for myself; I fought him for the entire neighborhood. And it was a good feeling. After I beat Corky, he didn't pick on anybody anymore.

For a while, I walked around the neighborhood looking over my shoulder. I thought Corky might come after me. But he didn't, and I was surprised by what he said to me when I did see him again. He told me that I was a good fighter and that I was going to go a long way. Then he shook my hand and walked off.

Over the years, Corky and I kind of became friends and he kept up with all my fights. After Ken Norton broke my jaw, I thought about Corky. I called up an old friend, Lawrence Montgomery, who had grown up next door to me back in Louisville. I asked Lawrence where Corky was now; I wanted to hear what he thought of my fight with Norton. But I didn't get the chance to talk to Corky. Lawrence told me that Corky was dead. Just a few weeks before I called, Corky was in a shootout with the police, at a bar on Walnut Street in Louisville. Corky Baker had still been fighting in the streets.

I still think of Corky. He reminds me of what can be accomplished if we face our fears.

Soon there was another obstacle I had to confront. This fear almost kept me from achieving an important goal.

confronting FEAR

The one thing that I have always feared is airplanes. It is funny when I think about it now, because if I added up all the hours and days I've spent traveling around the world for the past forty-plus years in airplanes, it would be a big chunk of my life. The first time I had to get on a plane was when I was going to the Olympic trials in California. It was a rough flight from Louisville to California and I didn't want to fly again. I told Mr. Martin that if I couldn't take a boat or a train, or get to the Olympics in Rome some other way, I wasn't going. Naturally, he tried to ease my anxiety, but as far as I was concerned, my mind was made up.

All I could think about was the terrible turbulence on that flight to California. I was so scared. I couldn't stop thinking about what would happen if something went wrong with the plane while we were in the air. If the flight were smooth, I would be OK, even though I still would wonder about all those buttons that the pilots would be messing with in the cockpit. What would happen if one of them broke, especially in flight between America and Italy? Then I worried about what would happen if, over the ocean, an engine blew up! Even if we didn't blow up, and we didn't crash, where would we land? Then, if we were in the water, would I be able to get a life raft out? If we did manage to make it into a life raft, how long would it be before we were found? And then, what if a shark came and punctured the thing? All of these thoughts raced through my mind. Even now it's scary when a plane starts bumping and swinging and I see the wings looking like they're going to break off. That's when I say to myself, "Boy, I should have taken a train or a bus!" The good thing about a bus or a train is that they don't fall thirty thousand feet when they break down.

For a while I was serious about not going to Italy for the Olympics, and then I thought about what my father said, "Always confront the things you fear." I realized that we are only brave when we have something to lose and we still try. We can't be brave without fear.

I realized that this was one of those important moments when I would have to make a choice. There are little choices we make every day that set the standard for the rest of our lives. But this didn't seem like a little choice to me, and I knew it would have a great impact on my life. If I didn't get on that plane, I couldn't win the gold medal. If I had not faced that fear and gone on to win the gold medal at the Olympics, I might not have become the heavyweight champion of the world. If I let fear stand in my way, I would never have accomplished anything important in my life.

Having made the decision, I was soon on my way to Italy for the 1960 Olympic Games.

the road <u>*to*</u> SUCCESS

I used to dream that I was running down Broadway, the main street in Louisville, when all of a sudden a truck was coming at me. I ran toward the truck, waving my arms, and I took off flying. I went right up over the truck. People were standing around cheering and waving at me. I waved back, and kept on flying. I dreamed that dream all the time.

After achieving success in life, many people forget what it was like when they were first starting out. Somewhere along the way, they forget what it felt like to look up to someone and admire them. I learned always to make time for my fans. This lesson was learned by a big disappointment of my own.

It was the summer of 1960. The Olympic team gathered in New York City, en route to Italy. I was eighteen years old and, for as long as I could remember, I had looked up to Sugar Ray Robinson. The night I arrived in New York, the sportswriter Dick Schaap took me and some of the other guys up to "Sugar Ray's," a nightclub in Harlem that Sugar Ray Robinson owned. Back then, Dick Schaap was also just starting out in his career. For some reason, he took a special interest in me. He showed me around the city and bought me my first slice of New York cheesecake. Then, when he found out that I wanted to meet Sugar Ray Robinson, he arranged a trip to his club for dinner.

On the drive up, I can remember wondering what color Sugar Ray's Cadillac would be that year. The last one I heard about was pink. I thought about what color mine would be when I made it big as a boxer. I thought red would be a nice color. Anyway, the club was on Fifth Avenue and 125th Street. I couldn't wait to get there. I wanted to shake Sugar Ray Robinson's hand and tell him how much I admired him. I thought that he was great.

Sugar Ray was the kind of boxer I wanted to be. He was talented, quick on his feet, handsome, and well dressed. Growing up, I had listened to all his fights on the radio. I used to jump up and down throwing punches in the air.

When we arrived at the club, everyone took a seat and enjoyed the music. People were always shocked when they found out that I couldn't dance. But it was true; outside the ring my feet would lose their rhythm and grace, and they wouldn't move to the tune. Regardless, I have always enjoyed listening to good music and, every now and again, I would get up and dance anyway.

I didn't get a chance to meet Sugar Ray that night, but I remember the address of his club like I was reading it from the outside of the building now.

As we were leaving, I noticed a man standing on the corner of Seventh Avenue and 125th Street. He stood out because he was holding up a sign that said "BUY BLACK." I had never seen any Black man in Louisville do something as bold as that.

Before we left for Italy I tried again to meet Sugar Ray. I walked all the way up Fifth Avenue to 125th Street. I wanted to get his autograph and tell him that I was on my way to the Olympics to win a gold medal. I wanted to tell him that I admired him, and that I was going to be the heavyweight champion of the world by the time I was twenty-one. When I arrived at the club I waited outside all day for Sugar Ray to get there. I didn't mind waiting; I would have stood outside all week if I had to.

It was about ten o'clock when he finally drove up. I was so excited that for the first time in my life, I was speechless. When I pulled myself together, I walked up to Mr. Robinson and told him how far I had come just to see him and how long I had been waiting to get his autograph. I told him that I was going to be the heavyweight champion of the whole world, and that he was my hero.

When I think back, I realize he never really looked at me. He gave me a quick pat on the shoulder and told me, "Later, boy, I'm busy right now." I was crushed. I couldn't believe he brushed me aside like that, especially after I had waited all day for him to show up. I felt as if my feet were made of cement. I couldn't move. I just stood there as I watched Sugar Ray Robinson turn his back to me and walk away. Although I felt hurt and let down, I decided that I wouldn't let my disappointment get the best of me.

*　　*　　*

I was going to be different when I became a great boxer. I would be the kind of champion that fans could walk up to and talk to. I would shake their hands and sign every autograph, even sign some autographs in advance so that when I was in a hurry, I could still hand them out to people, assuring everyone went home happy.

I was going to go out of my way to show my fans how important they were, and how much I appreciated them.

At that moment, I vowed never to turn a fan away.

I didn't want anyone to feel the disappointment and hurt that I felt that night. I was always going to make time for the people who looked up to me; especially children. I knew that when I became a champion—and I knew that I would—I was going to remember what it was like before I made it big. I wasn't going to forget where I came from.

I was going to be my own kind of champion, a champ to all people everywhere in the world. And no matter how high I climbed up the ladder of success, I was going to view the world without looking down on anyone. And I wasn't going to forget the boy that I once was.

I had a golden vision, but before any of it could happen, I had to win at the Olympics.

a

GOLDEN VICTORY

On the way to and from Rome, I wore a parachute that I bought at an army surplus store. My plan was to drop to the floor as soon as the plane started shaking, with my parachute line ready in my hand, so I could jump out and pull the cord if our plane started to go down. I managed to distract my fear of flying by talking a lot, and before I knew it, we were in Italy. When I got to the Olympic village, I walked around introducing myself to people and shaking everybody's hand. I even remembered most of their names. One of my teammates told me that if I had been running for mayor of the Olympic Village, I would have won the election. We all had a good time, and before long, I was an Olympic gold medalist.

When they put the gold medal around my neck, a boxer from Poland who won the silver medal was standing on one side of me, two boxers who shared the bronze medal were on the other side, the flag was waving, and the national anthem was playing. At the time I felt like I had defeated America's so-called enemies. I stood there so proudly for my country. I felt like I had whupped the whole world for America.

I looked at my gold medal and said to myself, *I'm the champ of the whole world, and now I'm going to be able to do something for my people. I'm really going to be able to get equality for my people!*

Before I left the Olympic Village a Soviet reporter asked me how it felt to win the gold medal for my country when there were restaurants in the United States where I couldn't eat. I told him that we had qualified people working on that problem, and that I wasn't worried about the outcome. I told him that I thought the United States was the best country in the world, including his. My spirits were so high, I wasn't going to let anyone or anything bring me down.

When we arrived in Louisville, it had been twenty-one days since I had last seen my parents. That was the longest that I had ever been away from home. I walked off of the plane, wearing my gold medal. My mother, father, and brother were already standing there, along with the press and a small crowd. I read aloud for all to hear what would be my first published poem. I called it

HOW CASSIUS TOOK ROME

To make America the greatest is my goal,
So I beat the Russians, and I beat the Pole,
and for the USA won the Medal of Gold.
Italians said, "You're Greater than the Cassius of Old."
We like your name, we like your game,
So make Rome your home if you will.
I said I appreciate your kind hospitality,
But the USA is my county still,
'Cause they're waiting to welcome me in Louisville.

As I walked down the streets of Louisville, with my parents and my brother beside me, I received a hero's welcome.

There were Black and White crowds on the sidewalks; we had a police escort all the way downtown; my classmates from Central High were there, and the mayor told me that my gold medal was the key to the city. It all felt so good that I never let that gold medal out of my sight.

I wore it everywhere I went. I ate with it, showered with it, slept with it. I didn't even take it off when the edges were cutting my back as I turned over in my sleep. Nothing could make me part with it, not even when the gold began to wear off. But, I did wonder sometimes why the richest nation in the world didn't give its champions solid gold.

When the offers for management started rolling in, I didn't pay them much attention at first, because I wanted Joe Louis to be my manager. But Joe was the quiet type, and he didn't like loudmouth, bragging fighters, so he turned me down.

Joe must not have thought I was much of a boxer. He even predicted that I would lose all of my professional fights. I guess he wasn't so smart after all.

My second choice was Sugar Ray Robinson. He was at the end of his career and I thought that he might be interested in managing me, but when I spoke to him, he told me to come back in a few years, he didn't have the time.

It seemed like the only people who showed any interest in me were White southerners. One of the first contracts I was offered was from Joe Martin. I was not offered any cash advance, only the promise of seventy-five dollars a week for ten years. Needless to say, my father ripped it up immediately. So I ended up signing a six-year contract with ten Louisville millionaires. They became my sponsoring group. I received a ten-thousand-dollar advance, and they received 50 percent of all my earnings, in and out of the ring. It seemed like a good deal to me at the time.

I was really happy about that ten-thousand-dollar advance. It seemed like so much money. Our house had cost forty-five-hundred dollars and it was taking my father forever to pay it off, so ten thousand dollars sounded really good. Everything seemed to be working out for me. Even though I often thought about what happened with Joe Louis and Sugar Ray Robinson, I didn't hold a grudge toward either of them. They both did what they felt was right, and we eventually became friends.

Sugar Ray Robinson was there to support me in 1964 when I won the heavyweight title against Sonny Liston. As I stood before all of the cameras and the critics shouting "I am the greatest, I shook up the world!" Sugar Ray was on my left and Bundini Brown was on my right. They were both hugging me and laughing while trying to cover my mouth at the same time. It's funny how things turn out in life. Sugar Ray later told me that he often wondered what might have been if he had been my manager, but I knew that everything happened exactly the way it was supposed to.

The last time I saw Sugar Ray Robinson was in his Los Angeles home. He wasn't well then. I told him again how much he meant to me and that he was the greatest fighter who ever lived.

Then I told him that I was still waiting for that autograph.

an
ACT | *LIBERATION*
of

The greatest victory in life
    is to rise above the material things
that we once valued most.

There comes a time in every person's life when he has to choose the course his life will take. On my journey I have found that the path to self-discovery is the most liberating choice of all.

My Olympic gold medal meant so much to me. It was a symbol of what I had accomplished for myself and for my country. Although I still experienced some of the same racial discrimination that I always had, my spirits were so high that I thought all of that would change.

A Kentucky newspaper wrote that my gold medal was the greatest prize any Black boy ever brought home to Louisville. I was proud, but I remember thinking at the time, if any White boy ever brought back anything greater, I sure didn't hear about it. It seemed that I had become Louisville's Black "Great White Hope." I expected my gold medal to achieve something greater for me. During my first few days home, it seemed to accomplish exactly what I hoped, but soon I had a rude awakening.

I was sure they were finally going to let me eat downtown. In those days almost every restaurant, hotel, and movie theater in Louisville and the entire South was either closed to Blacks, or had segregated sections. But I thought that my medal would open them up to me.

One day my friend Ronnie and I were riding our motor bikes around downtown Louisville, when it began to rain. We parked and walked into a little restaurant, where we sat down and ordered two cheeseburgers and two vanilla milk shakes.

I was so proud, sitting there with my gold medal around my neck. (I wore it everywhere in those days.) The waitress looked at both of us and said, "We don't serve Negroes."

I politely replied, "Well, we don't eat them either."

I told her I was Cassius Clay, the Olympic Champion. Ronnie pointed to my gold medal.

Then the waitress looked me over again and went to the back, to speak with the manager. Ronnie and I could see them huddled over, talking and looking back at us.

We were sure that now that they knew who I was we would be able to stay and eat, but when the waitress came back, she said that she was sorry, but we had to leave.

As Ronnie and I stood up and walked out of the door, my heart was pounding. I wanted my medal to mean something—the mayor had said it was the key to Louisville. It was supposed to mean freedom and equality. I wanted to tell them all that they should be ashamed. I wanted to tell them that this was supposed to be the land of the free. As I got up and walked out of that restaurant, I didn't say anything, but I was thinking that

I just wanted America to be America.

I had won the gold medal for America, but I still couldn't eat in this restaurant in my hometown, the town where they all knew my name, where I was born in General Hospital only a few blocks away. I couldn't eat in the town where I was raised, where I went to church and led a Christian life. I still couldn't eat in a restaurant in the town where I went to school and helped the nuns clean the school. Now I had won the gold medal.

But it didn't mean anything, because I didn't have the right color skin.

Ronnie wanted me to call one of the millionaires from my sponsoring group and tell them what happened, and I almost did, but more than anything, I wanted that medal to mean that I was my own man and would be respected and treated like any other human being. Then I realized that even if it had been my "Key to the City," if it could get only me into the "White only" place, then what good was it? What about other Black people?

Later I realized that it was part of God's plan for me that they wouldn't serve me that day. Before I was kicked out of the restaurant, I was thinking what the medal could mean for me. The more I thought about it, the more I began to see that if that medal didn't mean equality for all, it didn't mean anything at all.

What I remember most about 1960 was the first time I took my gold medal off. From that moment on, I have never placed great value on material things. What really matters is how you feel about yourself. If I had kept that medal I would have lost my pride.

Over the years I have told some people I had lost it, but no one ever found it. That's because I lost it on purpose. The world should know the truth—it's somewhere at the bottom of the Ohio River.

THE MIDDLE YEARS

Studying with Malcolm X, 1963.

To walk down a path
where great men have
been is an honor itself,
for a few privileged men.
But to blaze one's own trail
unequaled to thee;
Is a tribute to greatness
that few men shall see.

—*Anonymous*

the road to FREEDOM

Once upon a time, your great-granddaddy told my great-granddaddy that when my granddaddy grew up, "we would be free," and things would be better.

But listen, your granddaddy told my granddaddy, that when my daddy was born, "Now that we're free," things would be better.

Then your daddy told my daddy that when I was grown, things would "surely" be better. But they weren't.

So I told my daddy, that by the time my kids were grown, somehow I will have made a difference, and the world will be better.

Better far from all I see,
to die fighting to be free.

What more fitting end could be?

Better surely than in some bed,
where in broken health I'm led,
lingering until I'm dead.

Better than with cries and pleas
or in the clutch of some
disease, wastin' slowly by degrees.

Better than of heart attack
or some dose of drug I lack,
let me die by being Black.

Better far that I shall go
standing there against the foe.
Is there sweeter death to know?

Better than the bloody stain
on some highway
where I am lain,
torn by flyin' glass and pain.

the

FREEDOM
SONG

Better call on death to come
than to die another dumb,
looted victim in the slum.

Better than of prison rot,
if there's any choice I've got,
Rather perish on the spot.

Better now my fight to wage,
now while my blood boils with rage,
lest it cool with ancient age.

Better valid for me to die
than to Uncle Tom and try
making peace just to live a lie.

Better if I say my sooth,
I'm gonna die demandin' truth
while I'm still akin to youth.

Better now than later on,
Now while fear of death is gone,
Never mind another dawn.

There were many ways for people to participate in the Civil Rights movement
of the 1960s. Martin Luther King Jr. pursued peaceful, nonviolent methods

such as marches, sit-ins, and political organization. Some took up arms alongside Bobby Seale, Huey Newton, Eldridge Cleaver, and the Black Panther Party to defend, with violence if necessary, the rights of Blacks against those who would harm them. Others, like Medgar Evers, chose to work through organizations such as the NAACP, which used legal and political methods to advance the cause of civil rights. At the time, I chose to join the Nation of Islam, which promoted Black pride and independence. When I became a member, I was fighting for equality and Black pride at the same time.

Whatever approach you chose, the goal was the same: We all wanted freedom, justice, and equality for Black people in America.

Martin Luther King Jr. made a difference.

The NAACP made a difference.

Rosa Parks made a difference.

Malcolm X made a difference.

Elijah Muhammad made a difference.

I would like to think I made a difference, too.

black pride

I woke up this morning feeling good and black.
I got out of my black bed,
I put on my black robe,
I played all my best black records,
and drank some black coffee.
Then I put on my black shoes and
I walked out my black door . . .
and Oh Lord, white snow!

if I were | PRESIDENT

In 1976, I went to the White House to meet with President Gerald Ford. When I arrived, I told him that I liked the place so much I might go after his job. I was only half-kidding. I didn't want that job; it was too dangerous, but if I were president, things would be different.

During the sixties and seventies, people were always asking me if I ever thought about going into politics. After I joined the Nation of Islam, reporters were saying that I was involved in a power struggle. But it was never a power struggle; it was a freedom struggle. We weren't trying to get the power to rule White people. We only wanted to get out from under their rule and do something for ourselves.

*   *   *

Throughout the Civil Rights movement and the Vietnam War, I thought a lot about what America meant to me, and what it ought to stand for. Then I thought about some of the things that I would do differently if I were the president of the United States.

So, I wrote some of them down. I imagined myself in the White House, sitting at my desk in the Oval Office. I knew that the president would have to be White so I imagined myself as a White man ready at last to be fair to the Black people of America.

I would give an important speech to reporters gathered on the White House lawn. I would say:

Ladies and gentlemen,

It takes a real man to admit when he is wrong and when he is guilty.

We White Americans are guilty of many crimes throughout history. The worst crime our ancestors committed was bringing over those slaves from Africa.

I'll get to that one in a minute, but first, I'm going to stop the war in Vietnam tomorrow.

Start de-escalating, because we are leaving. I feel that it is wise for us to get out now!

South Vietnam, you must just do the best you can, because we're through.

Now, after all the boys get back to America, I'm going to tell the people who are getting paid for not growing food that they will get life in jail if I catch anyone destroying any more food. We need that food.

I'm going to hire a bunch of people with all those billions we've been spending on the war. I am going to pay them three hundred dollars a week to help their fellow human beings.

Furthermore, I'm going to say, "General Motors, listen here: I want you to make 50,000 diesel trucks. I'm going to fill them with canned foods and all the other goods people have been throwing away. We're going to take it all down to the Black people of Mississippi and charge them nothing for it.

I'm going to take all the money I would have spent on helicopters for Vietnam and it's going to go to Alabama and Georgia and Mississippi to pay for houses, nice brick houses with at least three bedrooms in each one. Every person who needs it is going to have a home.

Now, fellow Americans, all of you know that Black folks and White folks have had trouble getting along. We have tried almost everything from integration to sit-ins. Even tried swim-ins, and nothing has yet happened in a peaceful manner.

Black people today are educated. They're doctors, lawyers, mechanics; there's nothing they can't do.

Now, Black people, we're just repaying you. We're not *giving* you anything. We are guilty.

We *owe* it to you. Soon we will have a completely Black-and-White society, harmoniously living in peace. There will be no more hunger, no more unemployment. Everybody will be happy.

Now, my fellow Americans, I'm going to implement all of those plans tomorrow . . .

You know what happens the next day?

I get shot.

The president is dead.

SPEAKING OUT

When a man of great wealth and fame speaks out and tells the truth, he risks losing everything that he's worked for, possibly even his life, but he helps millions.

On the other hand, if he stays quiet and doesn't say anything, just because he could have made millions, he wouldn't be helping anybody. I loved freedom and loved my people more than I loved the wealth and the fame.

I proved that when I gave it all up.

the
JOURNEY

Our lives are a journey during which we must find our own answers and make our own paths.

On my journey I found Islam.

If I were not a Muslim, I might not have taken all of the stands that I did.

If I were not a Muslim, I would not have changed my name or sought to spread peace, and I would not have meant as much to people all around the world.

If I were not a Muslim, I would not be the person that I am today, and the world would have never known Muhammad Ali.

my

SPIRITUAL

evolution

The man who views the world at fifty the same as he did when he was twenty
has wasted thirty years of his life.

The Nation of Islam taught that White people were devils. I don't believe that now; in fact, I never really believed that White men were devils. But when I was young, I had seen and heard so many horrible stories about the White man that this made me stop and listen.

The press called us Black Muslims and referred to us as a hate sect. But that wasn't true. We never preached hate and "Black Muslims" was a name given to us by the media. This made many people very confused about what the Nation of Islam stood for. We declared ourselves to be righteous Muslims. We refused to take part in any wars, in any way, fashion or form, which took the lives of other human beings. We would not allow any government to force us to kill our brothers for political reasons.

When Elijah Muhammad said that White people were devils, he was mainly talking about some of the history of America. White people slaughtered the Indians, enslaved Black people and robbed them of their cultures so they had no real identity.

Elijah Muhammad was not teaching hate when he told us about all of the evil things the White man has done any more than Whites are teaching hate when they tell you what Hitler did to the Jews. That's not hate; that's history.

We knew that not all White people were bad and that there were Black people who did wrong, too. Some White people wanted to help us and in their heart meant us no harm, but how were we to know who they were?

The way Elijah Muhammad put it was like this: what if there were one thousand rattlesnakes outside your door, and maybe one hundred of them wouldn't bite you, didn't mean you any harm. But they all looked alike, so you couldn't tell the mean ones from the nice ones. What should you do? Should you open the door and hope that the hundred snakes that wouldn't harm you will come together and form a shield, protecting you from the other nine hundred snakes that want to harm you? Or should you close the door and stay safe?

Through it all, I had people of different faiths and nationalities all around me. My trainer, Angelo Dundee, was Italian. Bundini Brown, my assistant trainer, was a Black man, but he was Jewish. Gene Kilroy, my camp manager, was White. Ferdie Pacheco, my ring doctor, was Cuban. And Howard Bingham, one of my closest friends, is Black and Christian.

I loved them all and considered them my family.

I never hated anybody, not then and not now.

I was just proud of who I was, and Islam helped me feel that way.

My faith has evolved over the years, and I now follow the teachings of mainstream Sunni Islam. But, a part of me will always be grateful to Elijah Muhammad and the Nation of Islam for opening my eyes and giving me something greater than myself to fight for.

Changing my name was one of the most important things that happened to me in my life. It freed me from the indignity done to my family by slavemasters who took away our family name and gave my ancestors the master's name, like they weren't human beings—only property.

I have always been a spiritual person; God doesn't speak to me in a voice. It's more like a feeling, a sense of what I have to do.

Whatever that is, I'm in tune with it. The first time I felt truly spiritual in my life was when I walked into the Nation of Islam's temple in Miami, Florida. I felt like I had finally come home.

the day
I MET ISLAM

No one made me decide to become a Muslim. I made up my own mind. I was still in high school when I first heard about the Nation of Islam. It was 1959 and I had traveled to Chicago for a Golden Gloves tournament. The Nation of Islam was led by Elijah Muhammad, and what he and his followers were saying about Black pride really got me thinking. Their self-confidence and military discipline also caught my attention. When I went back to school, I tried to do a term paper on them but my teacher wouldn't let me because many White people, and some Blacks as well, thought the Nation of Islam was a pretty scary bunch.

One day in 1960 a Muslim minister—Abdul Rahaman, formerly called "Captain Sam" Saxon—came to see me. He was a follower of Elijah Muhammad, and he wanted to know if I'd be interested in coming to his mosque to hear more about the history of our forefathers. At that point in my life, I had never heard any Black man talk about his forefathers, except as slaves. This clean-cut, intelligent brother didn't have to ask me twice. I went to the meeting.

I saw a minister standing on a stage in a simple room filled with men, women, and children who were all dressed modestly. So I took a seat and began to listen. The things he said really shook me up. Things such as that the Black man was the original man on earth and how we 20 million Black people in America (at that time) didn't know our real identities or even our original names. That we were direct descendants of Black men and women kidnapped and brought here from Africa, and that we had been stripped of all knowledge of ourselves and our heritage. That we were taught to hate ourselves and our kind. Now, I had known this much about our history, but what came next was new to my ears.

He went on to say that's how we so-called *Negroes* had come to be the only race among mankind that loved its enemies.

Now I was a kid who catches on quick. I said to myself, "Listen here! This man is saying something!"

As I continued to listen, I hoped that nobody would ever hit me in the ring as hard as this brother minister was doing now. He said the Chinese were named after China, the Russians after Russia, the Cubans after Cuba, the Italians after Italy, the English after England, and clear on down the line. Everybody was named after someplace they could call home—everybody but us.

He said, if I say look for Mr. Chung, you look for a Chinese man. If I say look for Mr. Gonzales, you look for a Cuban or a Spaniard. If I say Mr. Weinstein, you look for a Jew. If I said Mr. Morning Star, you know he's a Native American. If I said Mr. Mobutu, you know he's an African.

But if I said Mr. Green, or Mr. Jones, the man could be Black or White. Because in slavery we were named after a White person. He was our master and we were his slaves. If his name was Robinson, we were Robinson's property and, therefore, were called by his last name. Our identity was determined by the names of our masters, and if we changed masters, our names changed, too.

Even my own name, Cassius Marcellus Clay, wasn't really my own. Cassius Marcellus Clay was a White man from Kentucky who owned slaves. So, I was named after a slave owner, and to me my name represented hundreds of years of injustice and enslavement.

The minister said that today we were all free. We didn't have chains on us. We weren't anyone's property, but we still had names like Green or Jones. He asked what country we so-called *Negroes* were named for. Well, *boom!* That really shook me up.

I didn't join the Nation of Islam right then, but the seed was planted. I attended a lot of meetings in different places and never came out confused by something I hadn't known or thought before. When I got more involved, Jeremiah Shabazz, the Nation's regional minister, came from Atlanta to see me. He asked me questions that made me think even deeper about my concept of Jesus, such as, if Europeans and Americans worshiped a White Christ why was it that Black Americans didn't worship a Black God?

I thought about my father back in Louisville, Kentucky, painting murals of a White Jesus in Baptist churches all over town. Who said Jesus was White? What painter ever saw Jesus?

I remembered that all the pictures on the walls of public places were always of White people. There was nothing about us Black folk. I saw little Black boys and girls straightening their hair so it would look like White people's hair. I learned that in Islam, God and his prophets cannot be brought down to the level of human imagination. There are no pictures of God or of his angels or prophets because no single race should be able to identify with God through the color of its skin.

I wasn't a member of the Nation of Islam yet, but whatever I believe, I believe, and I always stand up for what I believe. Before long I was in meetings, calling out just like the rest of the people.

Elijah Muhammad later gave me the name of Muhammad Ali. Muhammad means "worthy of all praises," and Ali means "most high."

The day I met Islam,
I found a power within myself that no
man could destroy or take away.
When I first walked into the mosque,
I didn't find Islam; it found me.

THE MEANING
behind the message

It's natural to want to be with your own. Bluebirds fly with bluebirds, pigeons want to be with pigeons, eagles want to be with eagles. They are all birds, but they want to be with birds like themselves. In nature, all the animals stick together with their own kind, so why didn't we stick together?

The Nation of Islam's main focus was teaching Black pride and self-awareness.

Why should we keep trying to force ourselves into white restaurants and schools when White people didn't want us? Why not clean up our own neighborhoods and schools instead of trying to move out of them and into White people's neighborhoods? The Nation of Islam taught that integration would work only after Black people had something for themselves. We didn't hate anybody; we just wanted to be with our own. Black people were in trouble; we needed to help ourselves first.

The slum wasn't in the neighborhood; it was in the heart and soul of the people.

We needed to clean up our self-image and love ourselves the way God made us. Then we could work and live together in a peaceful manner. Charity must first begin at home, and that's all we were trying to do—take care of ourselves.

God bless the child that has its own.

Well, Black people didn't have anything that was our own.

When I became a Muslim, I was on my way to entering what I called "The Real Fight Ring," the one where freedom and justice for Black people in America took place.

It's just a job.
Birds fly.
Grass grows.
Waves pound the sand.
I beat people up.

MY FIGHTING
HAD A PURPOSE

When you saw me in the boxing ring fighting, it wasn't just so I could beat my opponent. My fighting had a purpose. I had to be successful in order to get people to listen to the things I had to say.

I was fighting to win the world heavyweight title so I could go out in the streets and speak my mind. I wanted to go to the people, where unemployment, drugs, and poverty were part of everyday life. I wanted to be a champion who was accessible to everyone. I hoped to inspire others to take control of their lives and to live with pride and self-determination. I thought perhaps if they saw that I was living my life the way I chose to live it—without fear and with determination—they might dare to take the risks that could set them free.

I knew that my boxing career wouldn't last long. I had to be loud, proud, and confident. The world was watching and I knew that many people did not like everything about me. But sometimes all you have to do is breathe, and people will have an opinion on how you drew that breath. I couldn't live the way that others wanted me to live. If I had stayed in Louisville and never become a boxer, I could have died and it would never have made any news. But because I was boxing, and winning, when I said something people took notice. I had to use that attention to advance my real purpose.

personality

*Boxing made me feel
like somebody different,
and I didn't think it was bragging
to say that I was something
a little special.*

The majority of people have two different personalities: One that the world sees, and one they have in their private life. Some people think that my illness has dramatically changed my personality. They see me today as a quiet, soft-spoken, modest man. When they think of my personality during the years I was boxing, most people would have described me as a loud, boastful, arrogant upstart. The truth is, my personality really hasn't changed that much.

It's true that I don't *talk* as much now, but that has more to do with my illness than my personality. The outgoing and spontaneous person that the world knew while I was boxing was a persona that I created to sell tickets and promote my career. In my private life, I am quiet and reflective by nature. I have always been curious about the world around me and my place in it.

GORGEOUS GEORGE

LEARNING TO BE A SHOWMAN

When I was young, I never thought about the effect all my teasing and boasting might have on people. I was too busy selling tickets, playing around, and trying to promote my fights with my greatest asset—my mouth!

I never took the verbal sparring seriously. It was all showmanship, which I learned from one of the best, champion wrestler Gorgeous George. Not that I was ever really modest or humble, but when I was new to boxing, I did a radio program and Gorgeous George was on before me. That's when I learned how self-promotion and colorful controversy could draw in the crowds.

When the radio host asked me about an upcoming fight, my response was pretty tame compared to the one George gave about a wrestling match he was going to have in the same arena. George said: "I'll kill him; I'll tear his arm off. If this bum beats me, I'll crawl across the ring and cut off my hair, but it's not gonna happen because I'm the greatest wrestler in the world!"

That really made an impression on me because I couldn't wait to see that match. I didn't care if he won or lost. I just wanted to be there to see what happened.

Me, and a thousand other people.

I went to the match and he came down the aisle with these two beautiful girls carrying his robe so it wouldn't get dirty—real conceited, arrogant. And I'm looking at him and thinking, boy, he needs a good whuppin'.

I just wanted the other man to give it to him.

Gorgeous George was arguing with someone ringside, and the guy was yelling back at him, "You need a killing! You're going to get killed tonight!" Well, the guy had a lady with him and I saw Gorgeous George reach over and take the mug of beer from the guy and throw it in his face—got his suit all messed up. I found out later the guy was part of the show, but it was very exciting.

And I thought to myself, all these people are here to see this guy get beat. They all paid to get in. And I said to myself, this is a good idea.

So that's when I really started shouting, "I am beautiful. I am the greatest. I can't be beat, I'm the fastest thing on two feet, and I float like a butterfly and sting like a bee. If you talk jive, you'll fall in five . . ."

I started writing boxing poetry for the first time when I fought Archie Moore.

When you come to the fight
Don't block the aisles
And don't block the door
For you all may go home
After round four.

I won the fight in the fourth round, as I predicted I would. And over the years, seventeen out of twenty-one of my predictions came true. That's a miracle. I don't know how I did it. I started making predictions to sell tickets and my predictions started coming true.

When I said a fight would end in a certain round, it did. After a while people started coming up to me in the streets, saying, "If you don't get that man in the round you said, I'll lose my house, or I'll lose my car." Knowing that people were making bets like that, based on my predictions, made me nervous. But of all the fighters that I faced in the ring, Archie Moore was the only man that came close to matching my mouth. He had a clever response to almost every thing I said.

Like everything else I did, the critics had something to say about my poetry. They called my poems terrible. They said that they were the ravings of a madman.

I told those critics that I bet my poetry would be quoted and published more than any of the poems written by poets they liked. People who criticize usually talk about what they wish they could do. So, I never paid much attention to critics about anything negative.

Every time I opened my mouth, I could back it up.

The critics only made me work harder.

I talk to God every day,
If God is with me,
No one can defeat me.

MALCOLM X

A LEADER AND A FRIEND

I met Malcolm X for the first time in Detroit in 1962. I had driven up from Miami to Chicago to hear Elijah Muhammad address a large meeting, but Malcolm was the highlight of the evening for me. He carried the message that there was a special religion for the Black man. He was a charismatic speaker, and when he spoke, he could hold you spellbound for hours. Malcolm was among the most hated and feared men in America. I never understood how so many people feared a man who was only pursuing freedom and justice for his people. Perhaps it was because Malcolm was misunderstood; people usually fear what they don't understand.

Malcolm X was a man of great vision and pride. He had a good sense of humor and a quiet intelligence.

It didn't take us long to become friends. In time, Malcolm became my spiritual adviser. He started calling me his younger brother. We had a lot of good times together.

When I was getting ready for the title fight against Sonny Liston, Malcolm was especially supportive. I flew Malcolm and his family into town a few weeks before the fight. When Malcolm came to my training camp in Miami, he talked to me about David and Goliath. He told me that I was young, strong, and skillful. He told me that he knew I would win because time was on my side.

Malcolm helped me focus on my strengths and he strengthened my belief in myself.

I had worked long and hard to get Liston's manager to give me a shot at the title. For a long time they kept ducking me. Then one day they finally gave in. I'm not sure what did it, but I think I irritated Sonny's manager so badly, that he agreed to the fight just to get rid of me. Nobody expected me to last one round, let alone win.

Sonny Liston was big and strong. I believed that I could win, but I was still a little scared because of his reputation.

Sonny had already beaten the world champion, Floyd Patterson, twice—knocking him out in the first round once and taking just over two minutes to bring him down in the second fight. Liston was bad! By comparison, people were calling me a novice. The odds were seven to one, and they weren't in my favor. I figured that the only way I would ever get to Liston was by psyching him out.

My plan was to make him so mad at me that when the fight began, he'd be so unnerved that all he'd want to do would be to kill me. If that didn't work, I hoped that he'd think my behavior proved I was insane, and that you could never tell what a madman would do. Either way, I hoped he'd forget all he knew about boxing. I could take care of the rest.

A few days before the fight my sponsoring group and some of the fight promoters called me in for a meeting. Malcolm X and I had been seen all over together, and it was known that my cook was Muslim. People were talking, and Malcolm's presence in Miami made everyone nervous.

My sponsoring group still had me under contract for two more years and they must have thought that meant they owned me. They told me unless I sent Malcolm and his family home, fired my Muslim cook, and severed all ties with the Nation of Islam, the fight would be canceled and I would never fight again. So I said to hell with the fight and walked out the door. I wouldn't be who they wanted me to be. I was free to be who I wanted to be.

Later that night I received a phone call. The fight was still on.

I AM THE GREATEST!

Before the fight, I wrote a poem about how I would beat Liston. I knew I wasn't Superman, and if the fans thought that I could do everything that I said I could, then they were crazier than me.

I AM THE GREATEST

Clay comes out to meet Liston
And Liston starts to retreat
If Liston goes back any further
He'll end up in a ringside seat
Clay swings with a left
Clay swings with a right
Look at young Cassius
Carry the fight

Liston keeps backing
But there's not enough room
It's a matter of time
Before Clay lowers the boom
Now Clay swings with a right
What a beautiful swing
And the punch raises the bear
Clear out of the ring
Liston is still rising
And the ref wears a frown
For he can't start counting
Till Sonny comes down
Now Sonny disappears from view
The crowd is getting frantic
But our radar stations have picked him up
He's somewhere over the Atlantic
Who would have thought
When they came to the fight
That they'd witness the launching
Of a human satellite
Yes the crowd did not dream
When they laid down their money
That they would see
A total eclipse of the Sonny.
I am the Greatest!

7th HEAVEN

From the very beginning, this had been what I was working toward. All of the training, all of the sacrificing, all the cake and ice cream I had to give up. The golden gloves, Corky Baker, the Olympics, all to prepare me for this moment.

On February 25, 1964, I stepped into the ring with Sonny Liston and won the heavyweight championship of the world in the seventh round. I had just turned twenty-two, and my prediction of becoming the world champion by the age of twenty-one was off by only a few weeks. I knew that I must be the greatest, and I didn't waste any time telling the world. After all that talking and boasting, I knew that people were waiting to see me get whupped.

But I defied the impossible odds and shook up the world.

After the fight, Howard Cosell climbed into the ring and asked me if Angelo Dundee had given me my fight plan. I told him no, that I knew I had Liston from the first round because Almighty God was with me.

the black superman

A long time ago I was on a plane flying somewhere, and I wasn't wearing my seat belt. When the flight attendant asked me to put it on, I told her that Superman didn't need a seat belt. Then she smiled at me and said,

"Superman doesn't need a plane either."

I seldom told people this because they didn't understand it, but I never really had a fight plan. I have always trusted myself and felt like God was working through me. But sometimes I was so quick that I felt like Superman.

I learned early to feel my way along. I've been boxing since I was a kid and I have often relied on my instincts.

the
ANNOUNCEMENT

Malcolm X was standing beside me when I announced to the world that I had become a Muslim. People reacted by saying that I admitted to being a member of the Black Muslims as if I were doing something wrong. The press said that we were Communists, and that we preached hate. The next day at a press conference I told them that the real name of the organization that I belonged to was The Nation of Islam, and that "Black Muslims" was a media phrase.

What mattered to me is that I had made the declaration of faith that all Muslims must make in order to become a Muslim: I declare there is no god except God and I declare the Prophet Muhammad, peace be upon him, is the messenger of God.

too
LATE | *FORGIVENESS*
for

A few weeks after I became champion I learned that Malcolm X strongly disagreed with some fundamental principles that Elijah Muhammad was teaching.

For twelve years Malcolm X had followed Elijah Muhammad and believed everything he taught. Malcolm remained a devout follower of Elijah Muhammad, until the last year of his life when he went on a pilgrimage to Mecca and the Holy Land.

There Malcolm saw people of all colors living together in true brotherhood. There was no segregation. All the people worked together for the common good. He ate from the same plate and drank from the same glass as blond, blue-eyed, white-skinned Muslims. He came to accept that they were all truly brothers.

*　　*　　*

Malcolm now questioned the path the Nation of Islam was taking in the United States, and the leadership of Elijah Muhammad. True Islam didn't teach many of the things Elijah had been teaching.

Malcolm was going to separate from Elijah Muhammad and wanted me to come with him. He said it was important that I take his side so that I could become a messenger myself and tell other young Black people in America what was going on. Malcolm and I were so close and had been through so much, but there were many things for me to consider.

Elijah Muhammad had given me my name, Muhammad Ali. I felt that he had set me free! I was proud of my name and dedicated to the Nation of Islam as Elijah presented it. At that point in my journey, I just wasn't ready to question his teachings.

I was forced to make a choice when Elijah Muhammad insisted that I break with Malcolm. I was on a tour of Egypt, Nigeria, and Ghana. I saw Malcolm in Ghana where he stopped on his way back to America. He'd just finished a holy journey to Mecca that devout Muslims are required to make once in their lives, and he was wearing the traditional Muslim white robes, further signifying his break with Elijah Muhammad. He walked with a cane that looked like a prophet's stick and he wore a beard. I thought he'd gone too far.

When he came up to greet me I turned away, making our break public.

*   *   *

Turning my back on Malcolm was one of the mistakes that I regret most in my life. I wish I'd been able to tell Malcolm I was sorry, that he was right about so many things. But he was killed before I got the chance. He was a visionary—ahead of us all.

Elijah Muhammad had a mission to unite Black people in the spirit of racial pride, and he accomplished much. After Elijah Muhammad's death, his son, Wallace D. Muhammad, took over the Nation and brought me, along with many of his father's followers, to mainstream Sunni Islam. Malcolm was the first to discover the truth, that color doesn't make a man a devil. It is the heart, soul, and mind that define a person.

Malcolm X was a great thinker and an even greater friend. I might never have become a Muslim if it hadn't been for Malcolm. If I could go back and do it over again, I would never have turned my back on him.

COURAGE

Every man wants to believe in himself. And every man wants to be fearless. We become heroes when we stand up for what we believe in.

Before I won a gold medal at the Olympics, before I became the heavyweight champion of the world, before I stood up to the United States Government for my religious beliefs, before I was named a United Nations Ambassador of Peace, and before I became the most recognized person in the world, I was just a kid from Kentucky who had the faith to believe in himself and the courage to follow his heart.

the moment of TRUTH

The year was 1967. For months I had tried to prepare myself for what would happen if I refused to be inducted into the United States Armed Forces. I could continue my boxing career and remain the heavyweight champion if I went against my religious beliefs. Or, I would face certain backlash from the public and possible prison time and a fine if I stood up for my religious beliefs. That was my choice as I saw it.

The consequences of my decision were even more dire than I thought.

After I received notice that I had been reclassified 1-A, ready for duty in Vietnam, everyone around me advised me to accept induction into the army. This reclassification was very frustrating for me: I was now the heavyweight champion of the world, finally making some real money, and I knew that I wanted to use my championship status to demand respect and equality for all Americans, Black and White.

More important, my religious beliefs were not compatible with the responsibilities and expectations of a soldier in combat. I didn't agree with the reasons why we were in Vietnam in the first place, but most especially I couldn't see myself trying to injure or kill people whom I didn't even know, people who had never done any harm to me or my country. But even the Nation of Islam tried to persuade me to accept induction. I just couldn't do it. I didn't believe that was God's plan for me.

On April 28, 1967, I reported as ordered to the United States Armed

Forces Examining and Entrance Station in Houston, Texas. I was very nervous as I approached the building. I knew that everything I had worked for was on the line, and I knew that if I refused induction I was facing possible prison time. I had never been in trouble with the law and the prospect of going to prison was frightening, though I worked hard not to show it to those around me—certainly not in public. A curious thing happened as I waited for my name to be called. I looked at the young man who would call my name, and I saw that he was more nervous than I was. When I looked into his eyes, I realized he was just doing what he had been ordered to do, and that everyone in the room was just doing what he had been ordered to do, whether he believed it was the right thing or not. And suddenly I felt very calm and at peace with what I was about to do. I knew it was the right thing to do, and I knew it was the right thing for *me* to do. It gave me an overwhelming sense of freedom and certainty.

I refused to step forward. An officer warned me of the consequences of what I was doing, but nothing he could have said would have changed my mind. If I had to go to prison, I would do it, because if I didn't follow my true beliefs, I would never be free again.

Sometimes I hear myself described as a draft dodger. I did not dodge the draft. I did not run to Canada, and I did not hide in this country. I reported to the army induction center as I had been ordered to do. I asserted my right as a conscientious objector to refuse to be drafted, and I was prepared to go to prison for five years if I had to. I worked within the system.

After refusing induction, I distributed a statement to the press that read in part: "I am proud of the title 'World Heavyweight Champion' . . . The holder of it should at all times have the courage of his convictions and carry out those convictions, not only in the ring but through all phases of life. It is in light of my own personal convictions that I take my stand in rejecting the call to be inducted into the armed services. I do so with full realization of its implications and possible consequences. I have searched my conscience, and find I cannot be true to my belief in my religion by accepting such a call. My decision is a private and individual one. In taking it I am dependent solely upon God as the final judge of these actions brought about by my own conscience. I strongly object to the fact that so many newspapers have given the American public and the world the impression that I have only two alternatives in taking this stand—either I go to jail or go to the Army. There is another alternative, and that alternative is justice. If justice prevails, if my constitutional rights are upheld, I will be forced to go neither to the Army nor jail. In the end, I am confident that justice will come my way, for the truth must eventually prevail."

I never regretted the decision I made that day. Most people know that I was stripped of my heavyweight championship title almost immediately, and that state boxing commissions around the country refused to give me licenses to fight in their state. My passport was taken from me so I couldn't go overseas to fight. My prime boxing years were denied to me, and I had to find other ways to support myself and my family. The greatest cost to me, however, was that the Nation of Islam turned its back on me. I was no longer a member, and its members were not allowed to associate with me.

The Nation of Islam didn't make me a Muslim; my belief in God made me a Muslim. I found a spiritual home in mainstream Sunni Islam. My relationship with God is what got me through this period; it gave me comfort and confidence in the future that I otherwise would not have had.

THE BOY
inside
THE MAN

This is the story of a boy who lived inside of a man.

The boy and man were the same person, with one heart

but two minds between them.

When the boy wanted to run, the man would walk.

When the boy wanted to cry, the man would shout.

When the boy wanted to play, the man would work.

The boy and the man did not see eye to eye on much of anything,

except when it came to matters of the heart.

Both the man and the boy loved and shared alike.

One day the man decided to change his name
and the boy was scared.
He feared he would be forgotten or left behind
with all the other passing memories in time.
But the man reassured the boy that he could not be forgotten.
Because who he had been, and who he would become,
were one and the same, and they would always remain alike.
This helped soothe the frightened boy
and on that fateful day, both the boy and the man
learned what strength was made of.
At first, many people did not respect the man's wish
to be called by his new name and in the beginning
the man was defiant.
But the boy inside reminded him of tolerance,
and this is how they both learned what patience could accomplish.

After some time had passed the man grew wiser.
But the boy remembered all the sad stories—stories of other
little boys who had faded into memories.
So, he made it a point to hold on.
He focused on remaining strong.

Then, one day, the man was called to war.
The boy might have gone, but the man knew better.
He knew that if he went, the innocent boy inside—his better self—
would be lost forever.

So both the boy and the man learned courage.

After the man took a stand, holding onto his religious beliefs,

he was stripped of all that the world thought made him special, and

the boy became a survivor.

On that day both the boy and man embraced forgiveness.

For the man knew that if he did not let go of his pain,

their heart would harden.

Therefore, the boy and man moved on.

After much time had passed,

after struggling to carry on, the man was vindicated and his career

returned to him.

Although the man forgave, the boy remembered his pain.

Yet, through this ordeal the man learned

what faith insured, and the boy learned to endure.

Although the future proved promising and the life of the man

was rewarding, he would face many obstacles

and would continue to be tested.

And through all of the joy, laughter, tears, and pain,

the boy inside the man lived to tell the story;

He survived to share the glory.

—hana yasmeen ali

the
PEOPLE'S | *CHAMPION*

I never walked into the ring solely for myself. I knew that the people of the world were watching. I knew that if they could see a strong person who had also suffered hardships, but who had never forgotten his people or where he came from, they might recognize in themselves what they saw in me. I knew that the war I was meant to fight was a spiritual war—a war that would lift spirits and elevate souls—not a war that would take other people's lives.

When I look back, I see only what I have accomplished. The price I paid was nothing compared to what I gained. I lost the championship title. I lost three and a half of my prime fighting years. I lost financial security and public acclaim, but I gained something greater by giving it all up—

A title no man or government could ever take away: I was the People's Champion.

*A worldly loss
often turns into a
Spiritual gain.*

the presence of GOD

This is an old story that I like to tell. It comes from the teachings of Sufism.

Long ago, there lived a very powerful king. The king had a great warrior by the name of Rafael. No one within or without the kingdom could match Rafael's strength. He was the greatest of all the warriors. As time passed and Rafael remained undefeated, he grew very proud of his power, strength, and bravery. This made the king uncomfortable, so he thought that he should try to humble Rafael. But the king could not find anyone who could match Rafael's strength or courage. He was one of a kind.

Then, one day Rafael decided to leave the king to travel the world. During his absence a son was born to him. His name was Cushman. The child's mother died during childbirth, and the king took the child into his palace. No one knew he was Rafael's son. This was the opportunity the king sought. Over time the child became a great fighter. He was so strong and powerful that no one in the land could match him.

Then, after many years, Rafael returned from his journey. The king did not tell Cushman that Rafael was his father; he only said that a powerful warrior had come from far away to do them harm, so Cushman was told to fight him. Since Rafael's departure, it had become the custom of every wrestler to kill his beaten opponent if he did not surrender. Everyone in the land went to see the bout between two undefeated warriors. The king was sure that the son would conquer his father, and with great energy and strength, he did. But Rafael was so proud of his great power throughout his life that he would not surrender.

So Cushman took out his dagger and aimed it at Rafael's heart, whereupon Rafael revealed he was Cushman's father. Cushman fell at his father's feet, saying "Father, I would rather be killed than be your conquerer."

His father replied, "Do not let it grieve you, I am happy to know that I have not been defeated by anyone other than my own son, who is my own self."

What a change there would be in the world if we all recognized God in our fellow man. We may see him in ourselves and in our friends, but how much better if we could also recognize him in our so-called enemies?

standing TALL

If I had not been forced from boxing during the height of my career, I might never have known how strong my faith and beliefs were. The greater our level of understanding, the harder the tests become. The more we master the challenges, the deeper our faith becomes.

When I was stripped of my title and banned from the ring, I didn't keep faith as part of some deal with God where I would come out on top again. I didn't know what was going to happen or if I would ever be allowed to box again. But I believed purely and confidently that in the end, even if it meant going to jail, I would be all right.

When God is with you, no one can defeat you. I put all my faith in God, and in return he filled me up with courage and strength.

During the years I was not allowed to box for money, I opened a restaurant called Champ Burgers to support my family. I also took a part in a Broadway play called *Big Time Buck White.* The show didn't run very long, but I got great reviews for my performance and I had a lot of fun doing it. I still like to sing songs from the show, like "Black Balloons."

But what I enjoyed more than anything was giving lectures to people as diverse as brothers in Harlem and college students in America's leading universities.

I just put on my suit and tie, picked up my briefcase, and went out to share my beliefs. My lectures, based on Islamic teachings, were on various subjects. Some of the titles were, "The Intoxication of Life," "The Purpose of Life," "The Real Cause of Man's Distress," "The Journey to the Goal in Life," and, one of my favorites, "The Heart of Man." They contained important insights that spoke to something deep inside me.

In addition to the lectures, I would often share some of my poetry. My poems were not great literature, as my critics often pointed out, but they served my purposes, which were to entertain, to challenge, and hopefully to inject a little humor into the particular situation I was in at the time.

Following a lecture at Harvard University, I was asked to give a short poem. I thought for a moment and said, "Me, Wheee!" I learned later that the shortest poem had been, "Adam had 'em." Now, I had a record in poetry as well—for the shortest poem!

Someone jokingly asked me to become a professor of poetry at Harvard. I was honored, but I declined . . .

Pay heed, my children, and you all will see
Why this is not the time for your university.
It's not the pay, although that's small,
I have to show the world I can still walk tall.

the greatest

KNOWLEDGE

(TO MUHAMMAD ALI)

He's learned a lot, traveling around the world,
Being with all kinds of different people.
Little people, big people, wealthy and poor people.
Life has been his college.
The truth is, he never really learned from books,
But he sucks in knowledge, information, and ideas
Just like an elephant sucks in water,
And he trumpets it all out like an elephant, too.

—ANGELO DUNDEE

the HEART of MAN

There is a door to the heart of every man; it is either open or closed. When we value material things more than we value the well-being of mankind, the door to the heart is closed. When we are decent to others and share ourselves through kindness and compassion, the door to the heart is open. The greatest truth in life is that the happiness and peace of each can be reached only through the happiness and peace of all.

People look for wonders, miracles—surprises of all kinds. Yet the greatest surprise is to be found in one's heart. The greatness of a man does not depend on his material possessions. Regardless of how wealthy he may be, if his heart is not pure, he cannot be great. What most concerns poets are matters of the heart. Material things lose their value over time, while matters of the heart deepen and strengthen with age and wisdom.

The heart is resilient. It can be torn and mended. It can be broken and made whole again. It can rise and fall, and fall and rise.

What gives a person the strength to stand up for a cause, remain strong on the battlefield, endure all that may come in life? What gives us the power to have patience, and the will to endure? It is the heart.

Some people are so decent, loving and compassionate that the purity of their heart is almost visible. Some people have to struggle a little more to make these qualities a part of their being. Some people have to *really* work at just being civil. Some people seem to work at hardening their heart so that even the least bit of compassion or love won't seep out. I think, though, that everyone has the capacity for love, kindness, and compassion. But how much they allow those "emotions" to guide their lives varies significantly from person to person. In my own life, I try to allow these principles to guide me in the way I live and interact with others.

Service to others
Is the rent we pay for
our room in Heaven.

the
BLESSING

A long time ago, I took a walk down a street in Harlem in New York City. I came upon a man who asked me for a dollar. He had asked a few other people before me, but they only passed him by without glancing his way.

I stopped and handed the man some money. As I began to turn away, he reached out and shook my hand. He looked me in the eyes and said, "I will bless you."

Now, I'm not saying that was God Himself. But how do we know that it wasn't someone working for Him, walking around in disguise, just to see what we would do?

GIVING

If all the good that I have accomplished in my lifetime were measured against my intentions, I suppose I would have failed. When a person has been blessed with a life as full and rich as mine, he can never give back enough.

Some people give in order to feel good about themselves. They see someone in need on their block and they pity him, so they hand him some change. Others give to receive praise and that praise is their reward, but the purity of their generosity is diminished because they received something for it. True giving happens when we give from our heart.

Giving because you genuinely want to help a person or a worthy cause while remaining anonymous is true charity. That is the kind of giver I wanted to be . . . a giver from the heart.

I tried to teach my children never to turn a needy person away. I taught them to show respect for all God's creatures. I taught them to reach out to people who were down and lend them a helping hand. I taught them that by keeping the needy and less fortunate close to their hearts, they would be closer to God.

THAT
i s
WHY

Reporters have asked me many times why I think so many people around the world respond to me the way that they do. When I consider this question, a memory comes to mind.

It was a hot day in Miami, Florida. Gene Kilroy and I were driving to the airport to pick up Mama Bird and Papa Cash. As we pulled up at the baggage claim area a police officer recognized me and shouted out, "Hey, Champ, how are you?"

Then he said that it was OK for Gene to remain parked while I went to find my parents.

After a while another officer walked up and told Gene he had to move the car or he would get a ticket. Gene explained to the officer that he was waiting for Muhammad Ali to pick up his parents, that this was my car, and we had received permission from another officer on duty to remain where we were. The policeman told Gene that he didn't care who he was waiting for or why, and if he didn't move the car he would get a ticket. So, Gene pulled off and circled the airport.

By the time he made it back around, my parents and I were standing outside in front of the baggage claim area where I was signing autographs. As Gene pulled up again I looked up and noticed the officer giving him a hard time. The policeman told Gene that he'd warned him once, and now he was giving him a ticket. Gene hadn't been parked more than ten seconds. I noticed the officer looking my way. As they argued I walked over to the policeman and told him that it was okay to just give me the ticket.

After the officer gave me the ticket and we were driving out of the airport, I said to Gene, "That is why."

He looked at me and asked what I meant by that statement. Then I told him this story.

Two peasants were traveling down a winding road on their way to see the king. When they approached the gates of the kingdom an army of foot soldiers bullied them and ran them off.

Then one peasant said to the other, "That is why."

The next day, the two peasants traveled down the winding road again with hopes to see the king. This time an army of horse soldiers rode up, threw stones at them and ran them off.

Then the peasant said to his friend, "That is why." The two peasants would not give up, so they traveled the winding road again. This time the king's carriage pulled up, and when the king saw the two peasants standing there in torn clothes, with cuts and bruises all over them, the king got out of his carriage, walked up to the two peasants, put his arm around them, and gave them each a gold coin.

As they walked back down the winding road, one peasant said to the other again, "That is why."

When they were both back home sitting in their little huts, the other peasant asked his friend what he meant when he said, "That is why?"

The first peasant responded,

That is why they are foot soldiers, and that is all they will ever be.

That is why they are horse soldiers, and that is all they will ever be.

And that is why he is king.

Then I looked at Gene and said, "That is why the officer behaved as he did. Perhaps the biggest thing in that officer's life right now is that he gave Muhammad Ali a parking ticket. That is why!"

I always try to make time for the poor and the powerless, the young and the old. So, that is why.

still the GREATEST

Since I won't let critics seal my fate, they
keep hollering I'm full of hate.
But they don't really hurt me none 'cause
I'm doing good and having fun.

And fun to me is something bigger than
what those critics fail to figure.
Fun to me is lots of things
and along with it some good I bring.

Yet while I'm busy helping my people,
these critics keep writing I'm deceitful.
But I can take it on my chin,
And that's the honest truth,
my friend.

Now from Muhammad you just heard
the latest and the truest word.
So when they ask you, what's the latest?
Just say, ask Ali, he's still the Greatest.

the comeback fight

On June 28, 1971, the Supreme Court set me free. The decision overturning my conviction for violating the Selective Service Act is framed and hanging on a wall in my office in Michigan. With the change in attitude about the war in Vietnam, and the large amount of money that could be made from a boxing match between Joe Frazier and me, the nationwide ban on licensing me to box was eventually lifted. I had already fought three fights, not knowing if I would be going to jail while waiting for the Supreme Court decision.

The first bout was against Jerry Quarry in Atlanta, Georgia, on October 26, 1970. The day we arrived in Atlanta, I started receiving death threats and crank calls saying that I would be killed if I didn't get out of Georgia immediately. But nothing and no one was running me out of Atlanta. I had worked long and hard to get back into the ring, and the fight meant too much to me to just pack up and leave.

I wasn't just fighting one man, I was fighting a lot of men. I had to show them all that I was a man they couldn't intimidate. If I lost, I would have to listen to all the talk about how I was a bum, how I joined the wrong movement, and how I was misled. That's why it was so important for me to show them how wrong they were. I won in a third-round knockout.

My next fight was on December 7, 1970, against Oscar Bonavena in New York, and I won by another knockout in the fifteenth round.

Then on March 8, 1971, I fought Joe Frazier for the first time. I had been feeling like a caged tiger, and I took out most of my frustrations on Joe. I lost the fight in the fifteenth round by a decision. Joe had been too good a boxer for me to face so soon after I returned to boxing from the forced layoff of the previous three and a half years. And I did not count on his determination being as strong as mine. I wouldn't make that mistake with him again. This was my first professional loss.

I got my passport back in June 1971, and I traveled the world fighting professional matches and exhibitions, but I desperately wanted to fight Frazier again and take back my title. My plans were upset when George Foreman beat Joe and took the title. Now I was going to have to defeat both men to prove that I was the true champ.

My opportunity to fight Frazier again came at Madison Square Garden in 1974, and after a long time preparing to take him on again, I won the fight in the thirteenth round. While promoting the third fight with Frazier, the "Thrilla in Manila," in 1975, I did a lot of damage poking fun at him. I'd always given nicknames to my opponents to help sell tickets and make everyone interested in the fight. But with Frazier, I went too far and tension between us escalated until he really disliked me. The fight was truly brutal. Each of us was determined to win this deciding match, no matter what. Frazier caught me with solid left hooks. I wanted to quit, but I couldn't. I remember telling Angelo after I won that it was the closest I'd ever come to dying.

Joe made me fight harder than I ever thought I could. He was a formidable opponent whose skills I will always respect.

*   *   *

But I had hurt Joe Frazier in more ways than one and I didn't realize at the time how my words and actions impacted his family. It was never my intention to hurt them. For that, I'm sorry.

This poem is for Joe and his family.

THE SILENT WARRIOR

There lives a great fighter named Joe
who took his share of blows.
They ranged from high to low.
He traveled around the globe,
and walked the long road home.
His pain no man could know.

There lives a great champion named Joe
who kept his head held high.
He fought the best of men
and proved *his* strength would not die.

There lives a great man named Joe
who was belittled by a loudmouth foe.
While his rival would taunt and tease,
Joe silently bore the stings.
And then fought like a gladiator in the ring.

As the years passed swiftly by
The rounds diminished with time.
But Joe's trouble no man could know,
and his shame no man would find.

No matter how cruel the lyric,
No matter how painful the strike,
Joe was proud to be Joe.
His pride no man could take down.
His dignity rose with his crown.

Long after the final bout ended,
After the last bell rang,
News reached Joe's old opponent,
of the pain his family had suffered.

The blows weren't intended to hit home
But his family still remembers the anguish
Their hurt had never ended.
Now Ali could feel Joe's pain,
And Ali's sorrow could not be relieved.

So today Joe stands a great warrior,
marked with respect and pride.
For all that life has dealt him,
He never let strength subside.

The two men who fought great battles,
became blood brothers in time.

For every struggle that Joe survived,
For every dispute he endured, to rise.
Joe will go down in history
as a model for champions to come.

While Frazier was a man of few words,
Ali was a world of mouth,
but he found his place in history.
Now his heart can express him well.

Joe Frazier was a silent warrior,
whom Ali silently admired.
One could not rise without the other.

my golden FIGHTS

Of all the men I have fought.
Liston was the scariest.
Foreman was the most powerful,
Patterson the most skillful.
The toughest was Joe Frazier.

my philosophy

OF BOXING

I always believed boxers should not hurt each other unnecessarily just to please the crowd.

Most fighters are scared to lighten up during a bout even when winning on points, for fear they will be accused of being part of a fixed fight. I can remember watching other fighters and thinking, "Boy, I must be a fool. These two men are like two roosters at a cockfight whose owners have strapped knives to their spurs and had them fight each other to satisfy the crowds who bet on them."

I love boxing and it did a lot for me. But sometimes it made me think how savage human beings could be to each other. That wasn't the kind of boxer I wanted to be. My strategy was to be as scientific as I could when I fought.

I didn't want to be seriously hurt, and I didn't want to do that to anybody else either.

My plan was to dance, stay out of my opponent's reach, and use my wits as much as my fists. I tried to get into the mind of my opponent and psyche him out. I studied my opponents to learn their strengths and weaknesses, and to the best of my ability I tried to be completely honest about my own. That was pretty much how I won the championship fight with Sonny Liston, and how I won the title back in my match with George Foreman.

Muslims aren't supposed to trick people, and I try not to do that. I love magic, and at one time I was a member of a magicians' union. But because Muslims aren't supposed to deceive anyone, I would always reveal how a trick was done after I amazed everyone with my "magic powers." After I did this on a British television show, however, the magicians' union kicked me out.

Just as when doing magic tricks, boxing requires practice and dedication. Showmanship is a large part of both boxing and magic as well. I called my opponents names and boasted of my abilities and beauty, and often predicted the round of my victory to infuriate them so they would make mistakes. Some may call this a trick, I just hoped it gave me an edge.

True success is reaching
our potential
without compromising
our values.

TRUE SUCCESS

Success is not achieved by winning all the time. Real success comes when we rise after we fall. I am grateful for all my victories, but I am especially grateful for my losses, because they only made me work harder.

No one starts out on top. You have to work your way up. Some mountains are higher than others, some roads steeper than the next. There are hardships and setbacks, but you can't let them stop you. Even on the steepest road, you must not turn back. You must keep going up. In order to reach the top of the mountain, you have to climb every rock.

determination

THE POWER OF THE WILL

*Whatever the challenge was,
however unattainable the goal may have seemed.
I never let anyone talk me out of
believing in myself.*

A lot of people have disagreed with some of the decisions I have made in my life. Sometimes it has been pretty hard to go against the advice and criticism of others, especially when it came from those I admired and respected. My parents did not want me to become a Muslim or change my name. They knew that most people were afraid of the Nation of Islam and would feel confused by my joining them. They knew it would definitely make my life more difficult.

Everyone who cared about me—my friends, family, and fans—tried to convince me to accept the draft with assurances I would not have to fight or kill anyone, that I probably would just do exhibition bouts here in the United States. They said that if I didn't accept induction, my boxing career might well be over. And a lot of people thought I should quit boxing long before I did. If I had listened to them, I would have never won my title back from Foreman, let alone regained it a third time.

a newfound FRIEND

It was a hot day in May. I was at Fighters' Heaven, my training camp in Deer Lake, Pennsylvania, getting ready for my fight against George Foreman. After a long and hard workout I'd gone back to my dressing room with Gene Kilroy, who helped run the camp.

We were sitting there when there was a knock on my cabin door. Gene went to see who it was. A young boy with health problems wanted to meet me. I told Gene to send him in, and seconds later the boy appeared with his father. The boy wore a heavy sweater and a wool cap. I asked him why he was wearing that hot sweater and cap.

The boy told me that he had leukemia and that he was wearing the cap because all of his hair had fallen out, due to the chemotherapy that he had undergone.

A wave of sadness passed over me, and at the same time I realized how lucky I was to have healthy children. Gene took a picture of the twelve-year-old boy with me and as the boy prepared to leave I asked him his name.

"My name is Jimmy," he answered, and he added that I had made him very happy. I looked at him and told him that I was going to beat George Foreman in the upcoming fight and that he was going to beat cancer.

Jimmy gave me a hug. "You're right!" he said.

As the boy was leaving I said, "Jimmy, don't forget what I told you."

He gave me a big smile, waved good-bye, and walked out the door.

A couple of days later I had the picture of Jimmy and me blown up and sent it to the boy's father. On it I'd written:

To my friend Jimmy,
You're going to beat cancer. I'm going to beat George.
Love,
Your friend, Muhammad Ali

Two weeks later, while I was on the way to do my road workout, Gene told me that the boy's father had called to thank me for the picture. He'd gone on to explain that Jimmy was now in the University of Pennsylvania hospital and didn't have much more time to live.

This made me feel so sad that I told Gene to let the boy's father know that we were driving down to the hospital immediately to visit little Jimmy. Three hours later we arrived at the hospital and went straight up to Jimmy's room. When I walked in he was lying in his bed and I saw that his skin was as white as his sheets were.

Jimmy looked up with bright eyes and called out, "Muhammad, I knew you would come!"

I walked over to his bedside and said, "Jimmy, remember what I told you? I'm going to beat George Foreman and you're going to beat cancer."

Jimmy looked up at me and whispered, "No, Muhammad. I'm going to meet God, and I'm going to tell him that you are my friend."

The room was silent and we were in tears. I hugged Jimmy good-bye and later that night when we returned to my training camp, none of us spoke much.

I guess God had a bigger plan for Jimmy because a week later Gene informed me that Jimmy had died and that I was invited to attend his funeral. I couldn't go, so I asked Gene if he would go and represent me, and he did.

When Gene returned from the funeral he told me that there had been an open casket and that the autographed picture was beside Jimmy's head.

Jimmy's death was a powerful lesson in the midst of all the activity and preparation for my job—a boxing match—of how fragile and precious life is. We must always be mindful that each day is a gift from God that can be lost at any moment.

return *of the* KING

*In my youth, I set out to prove to myself
and to the world that I could achieve
anything I put my mind to.
This was something that I had to do
again and again.*

GEORGE FOREMAN

AND THE

Rumble in the Jungle

I wanted the heavyweight championship title back. In fact, I had not lost it to an opponent: It was stripped from me when I refused to go to Vietnam. I lost my chance to take it from Joe Frazier shortly before the Supreme Court vindicated me. The Supreme Court decision to confirm my status as a conscientious objector did not reinstate my title. There was no way for me to get the title back except to earn it in the ring. I thought I'd have to go through Joe Frazier again to get it, but in January 1973 Frazier lost the title to George Foreman.

Foreman was the meanest, baddest boxer on the planet. He threw hard punches and always came off as tough and serious. He was also younger and stronger than I was. People thought I didn't have a prayer against Foreman; all my friends and trainers thought I was going to get beat up pretty bad, some even thought I was going to be killed. But as a scientific boxer, I had devised a plan—a plan I didn't share with anyone—on how to deal with Foreman.

I watched a lot of tapes of Foreman's fights. I studied his strengths and weaknesses and made myself aware of how he fought. I also considered my own strengths and weaknesses, and then I thought about how I could use this knowledge to my advantage during the fight. I knew that Foreman was just too big and strong for me to take him on toe-to-toe, so I decided that the only way I could win was to tire him out. I believed in myself, I believed I could do it. I prayed and prayed, and I knew that only God controls the universe: I'd do everything I could and leave the rest up to Him.

It was decided that we would fight in Zaire, a country that was little known to Americans at that time. It was a country controlled by Mobutu Sese Seko, who was later forced to go into exile in 1997 when Zaire experienced a revolution and became the Democratic Republic of Congo. Mobutu wanted to gain attention for his country and the Zairian people by staging my heavyweight comeback fight at a stadium in Kinshasa, the capital. I thought this was a great idea, because here was a country run and operated by Black people: They had their own airline, their own post offices, their own supermarkets, and I thought it was just about the best thing I'd ever seen. A country run by Blacks!

I loved the people in Zaire so much, and they were great to me, too. I've never received such an outpouring of love and support as I got from them. People lined up on the streets to see me, and I loved interacting with them and learning about their lives. I spent a lot of time with the Zairian people because we shared a mutual respect. And I know that it psyched out Foreman; it probably made him mad that I was the People's Champ even halfway around the world in Zaire. He couldn't stand it when the crowds in the stadium on the night of our bout were yelling, "Ali, bomaye!" which means "Ali, kill him!"

Of course I didn't want to kill him, but I did want to win. When the bell rang I went right up to Foreman and punched him in the head as hard as I could, and then hit the ropes. I wore him out and beat him with an eighth-round KO. I had reclaimed the World Heavyweight Championship. Foreman was a sore loser at the time, blaming my win on everything he could think of, because he just couldn't believe someone as loud and pretty as me could beat him. He didn't know what it felt like to be defeated. But then he turned his life around when he brought God into it; he even became a minister. George has said some very nice things about me and calls me occasionally just to see how I'm doing. I think he's a good person. He has been extremely successful inside and outside the boxing ring—and I use his grill.

After the fight, I returned to the presidential compound, where I was staying, about an hour north of Kinshasa. The match had started around 3 A.M. in Zaire so it would be on during primetime in the United States. By the time I got back to my place it was actually the next morning and I was exhausted, but after Angelo and Bundini and all of my entourage had gone back to their rooms, I stayed up and sat on the steps of my cottage. A group of local kids came by to see me. I'm not sure if they knew about my boxing or the huge match I had just won, but they knew my face and name from all of the posters and radio announcements. They expected me to entertain them. These kids wanted to be with Muhammad Ali the magician and jokester, not Muhammad Ali the boxer. I love children because of their innocence and their ability to make the best out of any situation, and being able to entertain a group of kids after such an emotional and stressful night was really great. As much as the championship meant to me, I won't ever forget sitting up with those kids that day, doing magic tricks well into the morning.

champions to come

One day I won't be around to answer people's questions, or advise young aspiring athletes. What I want to say is for the people whom I've never met. It is for the boys and girls whose hands I will never hold. It is for the champions to come. These comments are for every spirit on the downside of advantage.

Champions aren't made in gyms. Champions are made from something deep inside—a desire, a dream, and a vision. They have to have the skill and the will.

But the will must be stronger than the skill.

When I was boxing I would set a goal for myself to demonstrate to other people what could be done, and to prove to myself that anything was possible when I set a goal then worked to achieve it. We create our own realities according to our thoughts and beliefs. The critics who told me what I couldn't do didn't know as well as I what I was capable of.

Everyone wins and everyone loses every now and again. If we didn't experience a loss we would never know what we are capable of. The important thing to remember is:

You don't really lose when you fight for what you believe in. You lose when you fail to fight for what you care about.

*   *   *

I'm going to share a little secret with you. Running has always been a source of my stamina. Early in my career I learned to run until I was tired, then run even more after that. But all the running I did before the fatigue and pain was just the introduction to my workout. The real conditioning began when the pain set in. That was when it was time to start pushing. That was when I would count every mile as extra strength and stamina.

What counts in the ring is what you can do after you're exhausted. The same is true of life.

Outrun the people who quit when they feel discomfort, outrun the people who stop because of despair, outrun the people who are delayed because of prejudice, outrun the people who surrender to failure, and outrun the opponent who loses sight of the goal. Because if you want to win, the will can never retire, the race can never stop, and faith can never weaken.

no sad GOODBYES

All my life I achieved the impossible by defying the odds, so after I lost to Larry Holmes in October 1980, I gave it one more shot. I fought Trevor Berbick in the Bahamas on December 11, 1981. I lost in the tenth round. Before the fight I remember telling the critics that I thought forty was a fun age, life was just beginning.

Age was mind over matter—as long as you don't mind, it doesn't matter.

After I lost my last fight I had to admit that it was over. Time had finally caught up with me. I would later discover that I already had Parkinson's disease. Before that point, I could never really say goodbye to boxing, so boxing said goodbye to me. None of the Black boxers before me got out when they were on top. I wanted to be the first. The truth is if I won my last fight I would have kept going. I would have been sixty years old still trying to achieve the impossible. Someone wrote that I stayed in the game too long and what I loved ended up destroying me. But if I could do it all again, I would do it exactly the same. Whatever I suffered physically was worth what I have accomplished in life. My heart told me one thing and my mind told me another. And when I had to decide between them, I chose to follow my heart.

My toughest opponent has always been me.

THE
SHADOW DANCE

The legendary fight that the world will never see
for the title of "The Greatest" is between
Cassius Clay and Muhammad Ali.
But if only for a moment this fight would be,
Who would win the Rumble between the
Butterfly and the Bee . . . ?

MUHAMMAD ALI (VS.) CASSIUS CLAY

Every time I look in the mirror,
I see that kid from Louisville, Kentucky,
staring back at me.
His name was Cassius Clay.

The kid says he is greater than Muhammad Ali. He claims to have made me who I am today. So I tell him that he is crazy. I look him in the eyes and declare that it was Muhammad Ali who made *him* great.

I insist that it was Muhammad Ali, not Cassius Clay, who stood up to the mighty government for his beliefs.

I tell him that it was Muhammad Ali who weathered the storms and endured the pain.

I tell him that it was Muhammad Ali who mastered the art of faith; Muhammad Ali, not Cassius Clay, who spread the truth.

Then I tell the kid that he was good—possibly even great—but that it was Muhammad Ali who invented the rope-a-dope and lit the Olympic torch.

I tell him that it was Muhammad Ali who shocked the world and made a place in history.

When I am through, the kid has a few words for me.

He looks into my eyes and confidently replies: "Almost everything you say is true. Muhammad Ali may have mastered the game, but it was Cassius Clay who dreamed the dream. Cassius Clay who inspired Ali to follow his heart. While Muhammad played the rope-a-dope game, it was Cassius who danced around the ring, shuffling and floating as if in a dream."

So, when you accept the awards and receive the praise, he tells me, remember one thing: It may be Muhammad Ali who is the greatest, but it was Cassius Clay who paved the way.

THE
DECISION

As Cassius and Ali danced around the ring,
reliving the dream, in the final round it came to a draw.
One could not be greater than what the other proclaimed.
From the very beginning they shared the same heart,
This has been true from the very start.

—HANA YASMEEN ALI

HAPPY MEMORIES

Not long ago, someone asked me what I missed the most about boxing. They wanted to know the things I thought about when I revisited yesterday.

Some days when I rise, I have memories of yesterday on my mind, memories of the struggles and challenges. Memories of the dance, the glory, and the dream.

I remember Angelo's shouts, Howard's flash capturing moments in time, and the sparkle in Bundini's eyes. I remember jogging with my brother at my side, and all the roads we traveled together. I remember the training camp at Deer Lake in the spring, and the smell of chopped wood. I remember the climb up Agony Hill and the trip back down.

I recall the roaring of the crowd and the sound of the bell. I remember the feeling of the ring, the dancing, the shuffling, the rhythm, and my speed. I remember the rope-a-dope and its victory, but most of all I remember living freely.

As life moves forward, I think of the pride of the crown; it all went by so quickly, like a sea of passing clouds. We have but a moment with youth, and although much has changed with time, I remember when I was king, and there are no sad goodbyes, only happy memories.

When I'm Gone

THEY'LL HAVE TO SAY

Someone told me once that thousands of years from now, people will still remember my name and tell of what I did.

When I'm gone, they'll just have to look at the records and look at my actions. Then it is up to the people to rank me where they want. They will think what they will, but my record speaks for itself.

They'll have to say I was the fastest heavyweight that ever lived. They'll have to say that I was the best looking—my face was unscratched and unmarked. They'll have to say that I was the most entertaining and the most clever. They'll say that even without a college education, I was smart enough to lecture at colleges and debate the best minds on television. They'll have to say that I was the only real *world* champion. I fought in such diverse places as Zaire, England, Indonesia, Switzerland, Japan, and the Philippines. They'll have to say that I was the most famous man in the world, the most famous fighter in history. They'll have to say that I invented the rope-a-dope and the Ali shuffle. They'll have to say that I was the boxer who could predict the winning rounds of my fights. They'll have to say that I was the People's Champion. They'll have to say that after I stopped boxing, the sport lost its zest and wide appeal. They'll have to say that I loved the people as much as they loved me.

And after they review all the facts, they'll have no choice but to conclude that I AM the Greatest of All Time!

(Not bad for a skinny kid from Louisville, huh?)

the world's GREATEST

I have said that I am the greatest. In truth, only God is the Greatest. But no matter what I had chosen to do with my life, with God's help I believe that I would have been the best at it.

If I had been a garbageman, I would have picked up more trash quicker and neater than anyone else ever had. If I'd been a reporter who got the chance to spend the day with Muhammed Ali, before I came to the interview, I would have thought long and hard about all the other reporters who had interviewed him before me. I would have reviewed all of their stories so that I could get a different perspective.

After my research was complete, I would have thought some more about what it must be like to be someone that was so controversial. Someone that a lot of people had once hated, but have now come to love. I would have thought about all of the pressures and sacrifices that went along with that kind of responsibility.

Then, after I came up with one really good question—I would have taken my question and worked on developing it so it could inspire a really great answer.

I would ask myself to reveal the most important secret of Ali's success that has never been shared before.

Then I would answer, first stating the obvious: God. Then I would name the following things, "It is the heart that makes a man great—his intentions, his thoughts, and his convictions."

I would tell my reporter-self that while I was proud, I practiced humility; while I was tough, I showed compassion; and while I was firm, I was also forgiving. When all is said and done, these are the things that truly count. They are what I hope people will remember about me.

I would tell him, off the record, "There will come a day when my records will be broken. There might even be a fighter as fast and pretty as me (maybe my daughter Laila—she shook up the world, too)." Then I would go on: "The one thing that I feel made me great wasn't my speed or agility. It wasn't the rope-a-dope or even my three heavyweight championship titles. For me, it was the prayer before every fight, the strength and focus that God gave me."

THE CURRENT YEARS

My family at my fiftieth birthday party.
Front row: Muhammad Jr., Odessa (Mama Bird), Lonnie and I holding Asaad.
Back row: Miya, Khaliah, Rasheda, Maryum, Hana, Laila, Jamillah.

*The body and the mind are only vehicles
    for experiencing life.
This realization helps me to live with Parkinson's.*

accepting CHANGE

A NEW BEGINNING

Change is an inevitable part of life. The seasons change, our feelings change, our appearance will change, and our health will change. Life is easier when we accept these changes and recognize how every moment of our journey is an important part of the growth of our soul.

I sometimes thought that I would like to be a Muslim Billy Graham. But God had a different plan for me.

A few years after I retired from boxing, I was diagnosed with Parkinson's disease. As a man who spent most of my life developing his physical fitness and athleticism, this diagnosis was difficult to accept. At first there were times when I could push all thoughts of the disease out of my mind. Later, when the physical symptoms could not be ignored, there were periods of frustration and depression, which I had to fight as vigorously as any opponent I ever faced in the ring. The only way I could deal with this challenge was through my faith.

It was faith that restored my sense of purpose and self-confidence. My faith gave me back my joy and enthusiasm for life. I think maybe my Parkinson's is God's way of reminding me of what is important: for example, how we treat each other. It slowed me down and caused me to listen rather than talk. Actually people pay more attention to me now because I don't talk so much. As with every other challenge in my life, I counted on God to be with me through this as well.

A few years ago a man gave my daughter Hana a copy of an inscription that I had written for him in a book in 1976. When Hana gave the copy to me, I was surprised to read what I had written all those years ago. It read:

People often ask me questions
I cannot very well answer in words.
And it makes me sad to think,
that they cannot understand
the voice of my silence.

the voice *of* SILENCE

It seems strange that I have an illness that makes it difficult for me to speak and move the way I want to. Those two activities once came as easily to me as breathing. Now, I have to work hard at speaking so people can understand me. I sometimes have to think about the steps I take.

Some people confuse my limitations with brain damage. Maybe that's because there are those who have said that I stayed in the ring too long, and that boxing caused these problems. But that's not true. I would have had Parkinson's if I had been a baker. There aren't many boxers that have Parkinson's, and there are lots of people who have Parkinson's who've never even seen a boxing match, let alone been in one.

Some people speak very loudly when they're talking to me, some very slowly—or both. I'm not hard of hearing, and my illness has not affected my ability to think and reason. I just move slower and speak softer and less often.

But there's something that hasn't changed with time . . . . I'm still pretty!

Fortunately, I still seem to be able to make people happy when I am out in public. In truth, I get a lot of energy and pleasure from being around my fans. Although I'd like to be able to talk the way I used to and have the freedom to move around like I once did, I am comforted by the belief that all of this is part of God's plan. God doesn't make mistakes.

REMEMBERING THE SPEED

I moved much quicker in my youth than I do these days, but for all that quickness, I missed a lot. Parkinson's has taught me to slow down and take smaller steps. I have learned to move at a different pace. And I have come to appreciate both quickness and stillness. Although I hope that there will be a cure for Parkinson's, my prayers are for people everywhere who are suffering, no matter what the cause.

Every day is different, and some days are better than others, but no matter how challenging the day, I get up and live it. And it is the combination of will and faith that helps me do it.

the power of will

When our bodies are at work, We are servants.
When our minds are at work, We are ministers.
But when divine will is at work, We are leaders.

—*Sufi Wisdom*

FOLLOW
THE
LEADER

People who have been diagnosed with Parkinson's approach me from time to time. Some of them even travel to my home to visit with me. They want to communicate their fears and concerns; they look to me for strength and guidance. I don't have the answers to all of their questions. The truth is some of them are answering a few questions for me. I am also just feeling my way along.

I believe that there is a reason behind all things and not all of our questions will be answered in this life. This awareness and acceptance have given me spiritual serenity and peace.

When I am at home in Michigan, I like to take walks around my farm and observe the beauty of nature. One morning, while I was walking, I came across a trail of ants. As I took a closer look, I noticed that the ants were heading somewhere. They were all traveling in the same direction, following the ant in front of the line. I watched as they came across obstacles. There were rocks in their paths, puddles in their way, and the wind was blowing small branches and leaves around. But the ants continued forward. They went over the rocks and around the puddles. It took them close to an hour to reach their destination, which seemed to be a small tree on the other side of our driveway. Along their journey, I noticed how some of them had trailed off on their own and others had stopped.

But the majority of them were still following the ant at the head of the line. As I watched them, I was reminded of how great God is. There are signs all around us, most of which go unnoticed, but when we do pay attention to the little things, we witness how even the smallest of creatures have challenges and obstacles to overcome, and then our own don't seem so insurmountable.

We are all so small in the scheme of God's grand universe. When I am traveling in an airplane, I like to watch the ground as the plane takes off. I notice how the houses and cars become smaller the higher we rise, until everything appears to be the size of the ants. We feel big and important here on the surface of the earth, but every so often, when we get the chance to view the world from a different angle, we can see things as they really are. It is during these times that I am reminded of what is important in life. There are thousands of people around the world diagnosed with Parkinson's and other illnesses every day. I know that a lot of them look up to me for guidance; they count on me to be strong. Knowing this gives me some of the strength I need to keep going. It is one of the reasons I continue traveling, and making appearances around the world. By living my life publicly, I hope to show people who are suffering from illnesses of any kind that they don't have to hide or be ashamed.

When I was first diagnosed with Parkinson's, I didn't know what direction my life would take. I didn't like the idea of being dependent on medications. For a while, I refused to take my medicine consistently. I even went through a period where I wouldn't do television interviews, mainly because I didn't want people feeling sorry for me, and I didn't want to let my fans down. My shaking and soft speech were harder for me to accept in the beginning. After a while, I began to realize that how I handled my illness had an effect on other people suffering from Parkinson's and other illnesses. Knowing that they counted on me gave me strength. And I realized again that I need people as much as they need me. I am as much at peace as I have ever been and I don't feel sorry for myself, so I don't want anyone else to feel sorry for me. What ever the future holds, I will come out on top.

I am like that little ant in the front of the line; a lot of other ants depend on me, and they follow me. Likewise I depend on God to give me guidance so I will know where to go.

When Ali first met him,
Parkinson's was grinning.
But Ali wouldn't go down easily.
Now Parkinson's is scared,
But it can't run,
And it can't hide
From this determined man
Asserting his hope and pride.

—Dr. Abe Lieberman

One of the nicest things that I ever heard a person say about me, came from Dick Gregory . . .

the representative
OF FAITH AND LOVE

(TO MUHAMMAD ALI)

Ali injected God into the arena. Whenever you saw Ali at the end of a fight, before he said anything else he would give all praise to God. He injected Religion. He injected Faith. He injected Belief. And that turned my grandmother on and my great-grandmother on. Even though he was a Muslim, he turned on the Baptist church and church people like nobody had ever turned them on before.

And I'll tell you something else. If people from outer space came to Earth and we had to give them one representative of our species to show them our physical powers, our spirituality, our decency, our warmth, our kindness, our humor, and most of all our capacity to love—it would be Ali.

—Dick Gregory

The Secret of God is revealed
Through the knowledge of Love

a higher
CONSCIOUSNESS

One thing that has always amazed me
is how many people question the
existence of God. They are always
searching for proof.

Would you believe a man who told you about a store that ran efficiently without any manager or salesperson to look after it? Would you believe that the store was protected from robbers without someone to look after it?

Suppose a man told you that he had seen a big factory where everything was running smoothly, without any owner or manager. Suppose he insisted the factory had been built all by itself, that even the machines had just appeared out of thin air and were now running like clockwork, producing wonderful products.

Or would you believe that an electric bulb could generate light all by itself? Could even the great philosophers convince you that the fabric from which your clothes are made had not been woven by human hand or by machine, but had woven itself? If we find these examples unbelievable, how could we possibly believe that the universe works so precisely without a creator?

Why does disbelief come so naturally to us, while belief takes such effort? Faith comes naturally to us in many areas of life. For instance, when a person becomes ill and is unable to treat himself, he goes to the doctor. When the doctor explains the cause of his illness and the method of treatment, the patient trusts the doctor and takes his advice. In matters of the law, we do the same; we take the advice of our attorney.

In education, we have faith in our professor's knowledge and field of expertise. We accept him and put our trust in him. We do this because we know he is trained in this profession. Belief comes effortlessly.

When we watch a car driving down the street, we know it is not operating on its own. There is someone behind the wheel steering it in the right direction.

Yet many people still question whether or not there is a greater power behind the creation of all life.

It is true that it is more difficult to believe in things that cannot be seen or touched. But this is the very essence of faith—believing in the things the eyes cannot see. Nothing bad will come out of having faith in God, so why not believe? You have nothing to lose, and everything to gain.

the evidence of GOD

In the midst of life's turmoil and
confusion, there are signs of God's
existence all around us on earth.

When it rains we sometimes see a rainbow. Moisture and light cooperate to create a stairway to heaven. We witness the seasons come and go in perfect timing. We watch as summer fades into fall, and fall into winter. Then we watch as the snow melts away and spring appears. Just as we trust that the seasons will change, we must trust that we can weather the storms of life. When God is present, nothing can prevail against us.

All we have to do is trust and believe.

how my faith
has
CHANGED ME

Islam has changed my life in every way.
It pulled me up and kept me clean
as a human being.

Islam has made me the man I am today. I do not drink alcohol, eat pork, gamble, smoke, or seek revenge against any other human being. Islam taught me that living a clean life physically, mentally, and spiritually elevates a person's mind, enabling him to see the world in a new light.

Some people hold on to hatred, revenge, and prejudice. But there comes a time in every person's life when he has no choice but to forgive or he will be consumed by bitterness.

We live in a material world that places too much value on possessions. Although I've been fortunate financially, my true wealth is within.

There was a time when I placed great value on the heavyweight crown, but that was before I had the religious convictions that I have today. One of the greatest lessons Islam taught me is how to recognize what is truly valuable in life.

WHAT IS REAL

If someone asked me what in life I considered real, I would have to say that for me, the only thing that is real is the spiritual. Only God and love are real. Pain, sickness, old age, even death, cannot master me because they are not real to me. Fame, wealth, and material things are empty and meaningless without a developed spirituality. We give them value and importance in our lives. But we must be careful not to value them too much at the expense of what really matters in life. Honesty, integrity, kindness, and friendship are the true treasures we should be seeking.

The key to peace of heart and mind is approaching life not with a determination to gain wealth and fame for comfort and glory in this life, but rather with a goal of realizing spiritual development. If you keep a positive mind and an optimistic outlook on life, negativity loses its power to make you unhappy. God's love is universal. He is with us always. Let Him guide you and you will never be lost.

fear

Many people said I was afraid to go to war. The truth is it was tougher to stand up for my religious beliefs against the United States government and millions of people who turned against me for my decision than it would have been to go to war. The government offered me all kinds of deals. They told me I would never hold a gun. They told me I would give boxing exhibitions and that I would never come near a battlefield. Even if this had been true, I still couldn't go. They wanted to use me to lead other young American men into the war. They didn't seem to realize that to take their "deal," I would have had to denounce my religion, my faith, my beliefs. But I was free and I was determined to be true to myself and God. If I had turned my back on my religious beliefs, my life would have been like a ship without a rudder on the open sea. Nothing could be more frightening to me than to try to live without my faith.

So they took my title, my financial security, and they tried to take my freedom. But they could not take my dignity, my pride, or my faith, because those were solid, real, and constant in my life.

PARENTHOOD

I tried to prepare my children for the challenges they would face as adults by teaching them what I've learned about life and religion. As parents we try to shield our children from the dangers of the world. We want them to have a good life, and we want to prevent them from making the mistakes we did. But although our children come into the world through us, they do not belong to us. It is our job to raise them and guide them, not control them, and to love them no matter what.

When my youngest daughter, Laila, told me she was going to be a boxer, I thought she was joking. When I found out she was serious, I was scared that she might get hurt and scared of the many other dangers she would face in the violent and unpredictable world of boxing. But she is independent and opinionated, like me, so I knew that she would make her own way. I told her that whatever she decided, I would support her. It turned out that she was very good. I tease that she got her talent from me, but I know that it takes more than talent to accomplish what she has. The hard work and determination were all hers.

Someone once asked me why I love children so much, and why I like to hug them. I told him that I always felt a special connection with children; they bring such joy to our lives with their innocence and sense of wonder. When I'm around children I feel closest to God; they are so open and honest.

I didn't get to hug and kiss my kids enough when they were growing up. Between the demands of boxing and the traveling I had to do to earn a living, I did not have enough time with them.

I've been married four times and I have nine children. I try to stay on good terms with the mothers of my children. Children must be free to love both of their parents and not have to take sides to defend one parent against another. Even though I could not live with all my children, I knew it was very important that I acknowledge my love for each of them and be available to them if they needed me. I tried to do this but I know I didn't always succeed.

*   *   *

I didn't have any children with my first wife, Sonji. Maryum, Muhammad Jr., and the twins, Jamillah and Rasheda, were from my second marriage, to Belinda. The kids were still young when we divorced, and there were weeks at a time when I didn't see them, even when we were living together, because of the traveling or training for a fight. After we separated, our children went to live with Belinda's parents in the suburbs of Chicago, and I visited them as often as I could. Sometimes I would watch cartoons with them on Saturday mornings. One of their favorite shows was *The Adventures of Muhammad Ali*. We would go out for breakfast and spend time just being together. Some of my favorite memories are of time I spent with my children. It seems such a miracle that they are mine.

I would tell my children that I loved them, and that no matter where I was in the world, I would be thinking of them and would always be their daddy. I think the biggest price my children and I paid for the demanding work I had was the loss of being with my children during too many important milestones in their lives, too many of the ordinary day-to-day times, when memories are built and life occurs.

Veronica, my third wife, and I had two children together, Hana and Laila. When Veronica told me she wanted a divorce, it was very hard for me, but we remained friends. In the beginning, I was afraid that when she remarried, some other man would take my place with the girls. I visited the girls as often as I could, but of course it wasn't the same as living with them.

I can still feel the pain and sense of loss from not being able to wake up in the same house with my children, and not being there when they got home from school. I hated being separated from them.

Even before the divorce, Hana never wanted me to leave. One time, when she was only five years old, I had to leave to train for a fight. Hana was crying and said something that was hard for me to hear. She said, "You're not my daddy. You're Muhammad Ali." She said that I was only her daddy when I was home with her.

In 1986, I married Lonnie, my current wife, who had lived across the street from my mother in Louisville. Her mother and mine were good friends. Lonnie and I have a son, Asaad, whom we adopted when he was a newborn.

After I moved to Michigan with Lonnie, we would fly all of my children to the farm for summers. We called this time "Camp Lonnie" because she did all the work, organizing and keeping it interesting. This was not an easy task; it took a lot of time and energy. But Lonnie did it because she knew how much it meant to me. Not only did we have my children here, but we also had my friend Howard Bingham's two sons, and two of Hana's and Laila's friends as well. I don't know how Lonnie did it, but I will always be grateful to her. Bringing all my children together, even for brief periods, was the best gift she could give me.

I have two daughters from other relationships, Miya and Khaliah. They were also very much a part of my life. I didn't want my children to grow up as strangers or to compete with each other. Sometimes I feared that because I was not married to the mothers of Miya and Khaliah, and because the girls never lived with me, they might feel less connected to me. This was especially true of Miya, because she has a lighter complexion than me and favors her mother in her appearance.

Because we didn't live together, Miya was teased at school and around her neighborhood. Khaliah didn't have the same problem because she looks a lot like me and Mama Bird. I remember an occasion when Miya's mother, Pat, telephoned me and explained that Miya's classmates and other children in the neighborhood were saying that Miya was not my child. They told her that she didn't look like me, and that they had never seen us together. So, I flew to New Jersey, where she lived.

I picked up Miya the next morning and we drove to school together. I sat through each of her classes, and when school was out we drove home. Then we walked up and down the neighborhood streets holding hands, so everyone could see that she was my daughter and I was her father.

A favorite dream of mine has always been to have all of my children living together in one home. I always wanted them to know each other, to be friends, and to love one another.

Each of my children is unique and talented in his or her own way. God has blessed me. I'm a lucky man.

DADDY

Because the demands of my career often kept me from home, I missed many of the little things that are among the greatest joys of parenthood, like being there for first words, first steps, first days of school. Of course, my separations from their mothers prevented me from being an ongoing everyday presence in my children's lives. Some of my children saw me more on television than in person, and spoke to me most often over the phone. I sincerely regret that loss to them and to me. I was not as good a parent as I wanted to be—as my children deserved.

I knew at the time I was missing so much. Now I know how much.

*   *   *

Whenever I could, I would record my children laughing, talking, crying, and playing. I would take a small tape recorder and capture the moments early in the morning as they got ready for school and ate breakfast. In the evening I would pick up where I left off and begin recording again, catching the moments when they were playing on my office floor or getting ready for bed. When we were together, I would have long conversations with them on tape. Because I did this so frequently, the children would forget the tape recorder was present. I have hundreds of these little audio tapes; they are my most cherished possessions. I often look at photographs and listen to these precious moments of my children's lives, when I was still Daddy, and so much still seemed possible. It all went by too fast.

I tried to be the greatest boxer in the world and a good parent, too. I had instant feedback on my success as a boxer. Often, parents don't really know if what they are doing is right or wrong until their child is grown and it is too late to change any of the decisions. Whatever my failings as a parent, I am very proud of all of my children. It wasn't easy for them to make their own way with such a controversial and public father.

FAME

One day I'm going to die, and in heaven it won't matter what job I had, how much money I made, or how educated I was. What really matters in life is prayer, living right, and doing good deeds, because this life is just practice for our eternal life. When people look up to us, even the way we speak to them can have a profound effect on them. I never wanted to hurt anyone's feelings or damage anybody's confidence, so in my private life—my real life—I tried to be especially careful about how I spoke to people. A word said in haste can have lasting effects. Some people tend to read a lot of meaning into the simple words that are said by those who have some fame. This can be good if people take something out of your words that helps them, but it can be harmful if they take something out of your words that can damage their self-respect.

While I always lived my life the way that I felt I had to, and not to please others, I still felt I had a responsibility as a role model for young people. I had to be free, but I had to do what was right. I was aware that many people—especially young people—looked up to me, so I abstained from using bad language in public, getting into drugs, or doing something to bring shame to myself and my family. I tried to live a clean and upright life not only because of the challenge of being a role model, but because it was the right thing to do.

When a man is a traveler, the world is his house,
and the sky is his roof, where he hangs his hat
is his home, and all the people are his family.

—Drew Bundini Brown

with GOD'S HELP

I always said that someday I was going to hitchhike from New York to California with nothing: no money, no food, and no clothes except what I was wearing. Then I'm going from California over to Asia and from Asia to Europe, and from there to Africa and South America. I'm going all around the world with just my face, to see how people greet me and take care of me. I think I could go just about any place in the world, knock on any door, and people would know me and let me in.

I might even march on foot through Venezuela, Israel, and the Sudan, all those countries, and tell people to stop fighting and agree on a peace that's fair to everyone. Some people say that might be dangerous, but you have to take risks in life. Columbus discovered America by sailing around the world when people thought he'd fall off. Men went to the moon by risking their lives.

And then, when my trip is done, I'm going back around the world the other way. And I'll buy food and clothes for everyone I met before.

In the ring I fought for my livelihood.
Before the government I fought for my religious beliefs.
In the world I fought for respect and justice.
Now I'm older and I'm tired—
But I'm still fighting.
I'm fighting illness, I'm fighting hunger,
I'm fighting poverty, and
I'm fighting for human dignity.
I've gone all over the world,
using this face that people know so well, and
fighting for peace and understanding.

A STORY OF
Gratitude and Generosity

My favorite of all the Sufi stories that I have learned over the years is the one about a slave named Omar.

Once upon a time there was a slave named Omar. He had been brought before the king with one hundred other slaves. From the moment the king laid eyes upon Omar, he knew that he was someone special.

The beauty of Omar's aura enchanted the king so much that he instantly made him his assistant.

It was not long before Omar gained the trust and confidence of the king, who put him in charge of his treasury, where all of his precious gold and jewels were kept. Many of the king's men became envious of Omar's new position. They could not understand why he should rise from a slave to keeper of the king's treasure.

Soon their envy grew into spite. They began to tell stories in order to bring Omar into the king's disfavor. One of the stories was that Omar woke up before everyone else in the palace and went into the room where the king's jewels were kept—and that he was stealing the jewels little by little every day.

When one of the king's men told him what was being said, the king responded, "No, I cannot believe such a thing! You'll have to show me."

Therefore they brought the king to watch in secret as Omar entered the treasury room. The king saw Omar open the safe. But what did he take out of it? It was not the king's jewels, but his old ragged clothes that he had worn as a slave. He kissed them, pressed them to his face, and laid them on the table. Incense was burning and the king could see that Omar was doing something important to him.

Omar put on his old clothes, looked at himself in the mirror and said, "Look, Omar. See what you were before. Know that it was not your worthiness that brought you to this position, but the king's generosity and goodness in overlooking your faults. So guard this duty as your most sacred trust, in appreciation of his generosity and kindness. Most important, never forget your first day—the day when you came to this town. For it is the remembrance of this day that will keep you grateful."

Omar then took off his old slave clothes and put them back into the safe. Then he put back on his princely robe. As he headed for the door, he noticed the king standing in the doorway.

The king looked at Omar with eyes full of tears and said, "People told me that you had stolen jewels from my treasure room, but I have found that you have stolen only my heart. Omar, you have taught me a valuable lesson. It is a lesson we all must learn, whatever our position in life may be. We must always be grateful, even for the hardships we have known. Then the king looked into Omar's eyes and said, "Omar, I may be the king, but it is you who have the royal heart."

RESPECT

It is said that there are two ways of dealing with people: One way is to control them, the other is to respect them. By controlling, you weaken the will of the other person. By respecting, you acknowledge the other's personal will. In one case, you make a person a slave, in the other, you make him a partner.

Long ago there was a wise man who lived among the elephants in India. He shared his food with them and slept near them at night. At the same time, there were men who were caretakers of the elephants who controlled them with spears and commands. The elephants usually cooperated with them, but when an elephant was mad, it did not obey the caretakers, and during those times the caretakers were sometimes killed.

But the wise man had a good relationship with all the elephants. His tactics were different. He would approach the elephants with kindness and ease, pet them gently, and speak to them with a tender voice. This is how he was able to sleep among them unconcerned, and in all of the years that he lived among them, not a single elephant ever harmed him.

—*Sufi Teachings*

UNITY

With all of our inventions and technology, with all of the planes in the sky, ships on the ocean, along with the discoveries of stars and planets, nothing can be agreed on concerning peace. When stronger nations begin to care for weaker nations, we will see unity. When people lend a helping hand without having to receive something in return, we will see humanity. And the reward will be peace among nations and brotherhood among men. When there is a crisis, tragedy, or national disaster, such as an earthquake, fire, flood, people set aside their differences and come together. We are like magnets, unable to resist the force that causes us to unite during such times.

God is working even in the face of catastrophe.

If only for a moment we could reach our original spiritual state of oneness, our heavenly and earthly natures joined; if we could learn to serve and love one another better, we would witness a better world.

recipe for a GOOD LIFE

Here is my suggestion . . .

Take a few cups of kindness
One dash of humility
One sprinkle of laughter
One teaspoon of patience
One tablespoon of generosity
One pint of forgiveness
One quart of love
And a gallon of faith

Mix in determination and add lots of courage;
Stir it up very well, spread it over the span of your lifetime,
And serve it to each and every person you meet.

Carrying the Olympic torch at the Atlanta Games, 1996.

THE OLYMPIC FLAME

THE SECOND TIME AROUND

In 1996, I lit the flame that opened the Centennial Olympic Games in Atlanta. I was honored to be the final carrier of the torch that had traveled across America, to be such an important part of the opening ceremonies. It brought back a lot of memories of my early boxing days, and I count it among the most memorable moments of my life.

It had been a long time since I had heard the roar of a stadium crowd. On the evening of the opening ceremonies, I waited in hiding behind the scenes as the events unfolded. Evander Holyfield carried the Olympic torch into the stadium, and he passed it on to the great swimmer Janet Evans. The whole process took only a few minutes, but it seemed to take forever. I had flown to Atlanta secretly a week before to do a practice run and work out the details, but I was still nervous. Who wouldn't have been nervous? Three billion people were watching around the world. *Three billion!*

When Janet carried her torch up the ramp inside the stadium, the whole world thought she would light the cauldron. Only a select few people knew that I would be the one. Part of the thrill of the experience was that element of surprise. When I stepped out of the shadows on the platform, into the bright lights, the crowd went wild and erupted in applause, gasps, shouts, and screams of joy as soon as they realized it was me, Muhammad Ali. Janet passed the flame to my torch, and then I carried it to a wick that sent the flame into the cauldron, high above the stadium. I could feel the waves of emotion running through that Olympic crowd as the flame took hold.

Watching the flame grow reminded me of my 1960 Olympic experience in Rome, where I won all four fights and defeated the European champion, Zbigniew Pietrzvkowski, and won the gold medal. Shortly after I returned to America I had briefly lost the wonder and honor I had felt as I first put on the gold medal, because I was still treated as a second-class citizen in my own hometown. Now the joy of the win came flooding back to me, and I thought about all that had happened in the thirty-six years between the two Olympic Games that have become important milestones in my life. I became a Muslim. I won three heavyweight championships. I refused to go to Vietnam. I traveled the world as an ambassador of peace. I had nine wonderful children. Everything flashed before me in an instant.

The Centennial Olympics reintroduced me to a generation of people who had grown up following my boxing career. Those Olympics gave me a renewed visibility; a whole new generation became interested in my life story. I had finally come full circle: In 1960, I shocked the world and won the gold medal in boxing at the Rome Olympics. In 1996, I showed the world that Parkinson's disease hadn't defeated me. I showed them that I was still The Greatest of All Time.

When the ceremony was over, I was given the torch to take home. Later that night, back in my hotel room, I couldn't sleep. I just sat there holding the torch in my hand until dawn. I couldn't put it down; it meant so much to me. Today it hangs on a wall in my office, so I can see it every day.

Lighting the Olympic flame was a major turning point in my life. Even today, people still come up to me and talk about their experiences of watching the opening ceremony and how they were moved by it. The love and emotion I get from these people gives me inspiration and energy to continue my mission of spreading peace and respect throughout the world.

IN TROUBLED TIMES

Praying with Prince Naseem, London, 1998.

ISLAM
AND
SEPTEMBER 11

Most Americans didn't understand Islam before September 11, and unfortunately, the tragic events of that day—and those who committed the unspeakable acts that caused them—have become the face of Islam for many in the United States. On September 12, 2001, I released a statement that said, in part:

As an American Muslim, I want to express my deep sadness and anguish at the tremendous loss of life that occurred on Tuesday.

Islam is a religion of peace. Islam does not promote terrorism or the killing of people.

I cannot sit by and let the world think that Islam is a killing religion. It hurts me to see what radical people are doing in the name of

Islam. These radicals are doing things that God is against. Muslims do not believe in violence.

If the culprits are Muslim, they have twisted the teachings of Islam. Whoever performed, or is behind, the terrorist attacks in the United States of America does not represent Islam. God is not behind assassins. Anyone involved in this must pay for their evil.

I believe these words as much today as I did when I wrote them. Some people blame Islam as a whole for the actions of a few people who claim to follow it. But they are mistaken in thinking this way.

Islam has two meanings: Surrender your will to God, and obtain peace in your soul. This does not mean that Muslims sit around and wait for God to do things: We, as Muslims, believe in doing good deeds, and that good deeds are true characteristics of our faith. Islam is more than just a religion; it is a way of life. We don't depend on doing good works in order to get into heaven; submitting our will to God is all we need for salvation. I believe that every time we do something good or bad, it is recorded and will be reviewed when God evaluates us on Judgment Day. Doing good work is one way that we achieve peace in our souls. We pray five times a day, which reminds us that God is truly the greatest and helps keep us focused on Him. We offer the greeting *al-salaam alaikum* to people when we meet them, which means "God's peace be upon you."

I do not claim to be an Islamic scholar, but I know that there is no room in Islam for those who would kill or terrorize innocent people. In fact, killing and terrorism are completely opposite to the peace that is so central to our faith. People who do terrible things in the name of Islam hurt not only the victims of their actions but also all Believers by damaging the true dignity and goodness of our faith.

As a Sunni Muslim, I look to the example of the Prophet Muhammad, peace be upon him, who respected and interacted with peoples of other faiths in his time. Muslims and people of other faiths have, despite some wars and conflicts in the past, enjoyed hundreds of years of exchange and interfaith discussions. The Prophet himself participated in such discussions when he was alive. The Holy Quran encourages Muslims to have meetings and exchanges of ideas with people from other religious traditions.

It is my prayer that Muslims and all people who seek peace come together and work to make our world a better place for ourselves and our children.

AFGHANISTAN

A MISSION OF PEACE

In 1998 I was named the United Nations Messenger of Peace; it was a title that meant a lot to me. Many people would be surprised to know that I have always been uncomfortable with violence of any kind. Being a boxer that may seem ironic, but it's true. I don't even like arguing in my home life, and when I was fighting I never tried to hurt my opponent. So when I heard the news, I was honored. I remember saying to myself, you're just an old man who left the sports page for the front page. But even so, it was another title that I could use to help make a difference in the world.

In November 2002 I visited Afghanistan on a three-day mission for the United Nations with the hope of raising awareness of the needs of the people of Afghanistan as well as the problems the country still faced following the fall of the Taliban regime. I had a chance to put my new title to good use. I was accompanied by my friend Howard Bingham; a business associate, Al Hassas; and my attorney, Ron DiNicola.

When we arrived I felt an instant connection with the country and the people. It is a Muslim country, and in spite of the danger and the destitute surroundings, I felt at home. These were my people, my brothers and sisters. On the first day of my mission, I met with President Hamid Karzai at the presidential palace in Kabul. An attempt had been made on Karzai's life only two months before our arrival. Someone had shot four rounds through his car window.

We walked into a beautiful room with a high ceiling, long, flowing curtains, and elegant chandeliers. News cameras were everywhere, along with dozens of security guards. President Karzai strode in with open arms and a huge smile on his face. He wore a long red robe suited for a king. Karzai made his way across the hall and hugged me. He thanked me for coming, and I told him we were happy to be there with press coverage so that the people of the world wouldn't forget Afghanistan and what was going on there.

President Karzai told me that he saw strength in me still . . . and that he wished I could stay with them there forever.

When I met with members of the former royal family of Afghanistan, I mentioned that I was thinking of buying land in Afghanistan. They said it wasn't necessary, that I could live with them and that they would give me the land.

I remember thinking about all the places I have gone, all the countries, all the events, all the towns and cities where people have offered me food and gifts because they loved and respected me. I've often thought if everyone in the world would try to love and help one another the way that they love me, the world would be a much better place.

The following day I visited a girls' school in the capital city, where the children had to meet in little white tents for their lessons, due to the reconstruction needs of Afghanistan. Under the Taliban, girls were banned from school and women were forbidden to work. I heard stories about how they had been stopped in the streets by Taliban police and turned away from school, unable to attend class. I thought about America and how spoiled we can be—how much we take our blessings for granted and how many of us squander them, like the kids who cut classes, create hardships in the classroom, and hassle their teachers. Most of them are unaware that there are people in developing countries risking their lives just trying to get to class. People and places like Afghanistan make me think about what's important.

I enjoyed hugging and kissing all the kids. They seemed to be entertained by the magic tricks I showed them. When I was through I showed them how I performed them. Islam teaches that we should not deceive people, and all those little children might have believed I was really making a scarf disappear if I hadn't shown them I was tucking it into a fake thumb.

It was hard for me to pull myself away from the kids. They were all so pure and innocent. I prayed that they would be able to hold onto that innocence in their war-shattered country. I hoped their future would be brighter and more promising than their past.

One of the highlights of the trip for me was a surprise visit to the mud-walled boxing club in Kabul. The club had two framed vintage photos of me as a young fighter in the ring. I handed out gifts of gloves and jump ropes. I was getting tired after shaking the hands of more than a dozen young boxers, but I found the strength to pound a red-and-blue punching bag for a few minutes as a small crowd cheered me on.

Several young men were sparring in a makeshift boxing ring, so I donned a pair of red gloves and stepped in myself to throw a few punches. I think I impressed them.

There are people taking stands around the world every day, but we don't always hear about them because what they do doesn't always make world news. So, I would like to share what I can to keep people mindful that there are unsung heroes out there who are fighting to survive. They continue to endure and carry on, proving that all things are possible when our will is at work. Upon my departure from Afghanistan I prepared a letter for the children and people there:

I want to share some of my feelings with you about how bright your future is. My life and my success were built upon the preparation that I practiced when I was a young person growing up in a poor place in America, and I know that you will succeed just like me if you can always keep these three things in mind:

Have faith and be a good Muslim. Your faith will help you through the most difficult days. Prepare your mind for the challenges of life.

Your education will be an important part of

your life. You must study hard, respect your teachers, and follow their guidance. Prepare your body by practicing physical activity and sports, because sports build fellowship, character, and independence.

I know that for many of you, it may be difficult to participate in athletic activities because you may not have all the opportunities now, but we must all work together to create more opportunities.

It has been an honor and a pleasure to spend these last three days in your beautiful country. There has been much that has been achieved so far in Afghanistan by the humanitarian community working together with the Afghan government and people.

Above all, I believe I have seen in the young people like you not just the Afghanistan of today, but the Afghanistan of tomorrow. That tomorrow will be your tomorrow, and the world must not fail you. This is where the adults of the world can make a difference to your lives by continuing their good work for the rebuilding of your country. I want to thank you, my young friends, for showing me how strong you are in spite of the hardships your country still faces.

You must keep the strength.

You must continue the hope for a brighter tomorrow. You are the life and soul of Afghanistan.

THE SPECIAL OLYMPICS

I have been a longtime supporter of the Special Olympics. In 1979 I helped open the Special Olympics International Games by lighting the "Flame of Hope" in Brockport, New York. And in 1998, I was happy to announce the Sargent Shriver Global Messengers, who are the worldwide spokespeople for the Special Olympics movement, in Chicago. So it was a great honor to have a recent opportunity to celebrate again the spirit and accomplishments of the Special Olympics at their thirty-fifth anniversary. The Special Olympics World Summer Games held in Dublin, Ireland, in June 2003, was a spectacular gathering of 7,000 competitors from more than 150 countries.

Special Olympians are *true* Olympians—they have overcome not only the odds against their becoming great athletes, but they have overcome obstacles that most of us have not had to face. Their first opponents—their own personal limitations, the routines of everyday life—were harder to face down than any opponent I ever faced. Once they overcome these challenges, they can do amazing things.

Nelson Mandela, the great humanitarian and former president of South Africa, was also in Dublin to honor the Special Olympians. I was so pleased to be reunited with this great man. He knows adversity firsthand, as he struggled against the apartheid machine in South Africa. Apartheid, the terrible, and often violent, institutionalized racism that for many years held South African society in its grip, was not an easy policy to fight against. Mandela understands what it means to fight against enormous odds: he went to prison for nearly three decades for his work, but he knew there was no alternative. He believes that every human being is of equal value. Nelson Mandela is a man of great personal honor, strength, and integrity, but he was always fighting for something greater than himself, and that was the freedom of an entire nation.

Like Mandela, the young people participating in the Special Olympics are inspirational, and can be role models for the rest of us. They show us that nothing is impossible. But I know that these Olympians use all their talents to the best of their ability and trust that God has a plan for them. That should be a challenge and an inspiration to us all.

meeting the
DALAI LAMA

A PRAYER FOR PEACE

I had wanted to meet the Dalai Lama for a long time. He is a sweet and humble man who works tirelessly for peace. As an exiled spiritual leader and outspoken advocate for the Tibetan people, he won the Nobel Peace Prize in 1989. He has made a tremendous difference in the way the world understands peaceful movements for self-determination.

We finally met in 2003 at an interfaith temple just outside of Bloomington, Indiana. The Dalai Lama had named the temple, which is on the grounds of the Tibetan Cultural Center, Chamtse Ling or "Field of Love and Compassion." His older brother, Thubten J. Norbu, had spent decades working on the temple in fulfillment of a long-cherished dream.

Leaders from sixteen religions and denominations were there to speak. The Dalai Lama wanted to impress upon everyone that "all religions have the same potential and capacity to serve humanity." He stressed that religious teachings should be a part of all of our lives. I understand that there are many paths to God, and I believe Islam is the correct path for me. Like the Dalai Lama, I respect people of different religious beliefs and agree that spirituality should be a central focus of our daily lives. Spirituality helps us

The Dalai Lama liked the gift of Howard Bingham's book of
photographs of my career.

achieve self-discipline, forgiveness, and love, which are so essential to a peaceful existence in living among others.

That afternoon, after the dedication ceremony, my daughter Hana and I attended a program for young people who had gathered for the event. Hana read a speech for me that we wrote together. It said in part:

We live in a world intoxicated by power and wealth. We have countries struggling against each other, nations taking advantage of weaker nations, men and women being killed, wounded, and uprooted by war.

With all that we've accomplished through history, we have yet to master peace. It is easier for most people to fight fire with fire, hatred with hatred, and injustice with vengeance.

There comes a time in everyone's life when he has to take a good look at himself and stop pointing the finger. We have to make an effort to be kind to others, even toward those we don't know. It is through selfless acts that we inspire change.

When a man is down, help him up.
When you pass a stranger in the street, share a smile.
When a person is in need, lend a helping hand.

Build your foundation upon faith. In life, there will be setbacks. There will be challenges, there will be obstacles. Sometimes you may feel as if your obstacles are insurmountable. These are the times you must be strong.

If you experience prejudice or injustice, keep your head up and your heart open. Bitterness will only weaken you. Don't let anger consume you. Never let resentment into your heart—it will only weigh you down.

I was grateful for the time I had with the Dalai Lama. I have come to understand that there are those who believe in God and those who make God a reality. The Dalai Lama is among those who manifest God in the journey of their everyday lives. Before leaving, I thought about how I would say goodbye, but then I realized that there are no right words. So I parted from him the only way I knew how—with a hug and a smile. It felt just right.

THE DALAI LAMA
and
MUHAMMAD ALI

Beside the great man there stands another
Whose heart prevailed against cruel winds,
Whose patience lasted without end,
Whose faith has refused to bend.

Beside the great man there stands another
Whose goal of peace for all mankind
He's pursued with body, heart, and mind.
Along the path of grace and thunder
Beside the great man there stands another.

For His Holiness the Dalai Lama
May you journey well.

—HANA YASMEEN ALI

THE SECRET OF MY SUCCESS

All of my life, if I wanted to do something,
I studied those who were good at it;
then I memorized what I learned,
and believed that I could do it, too.
Then I went out and did it.

HOW I WOULD
like to be
REMEMBERED

I would like to be remembered as a man who won the heavyweight title three times, who was humorous, and who treated everyone right. As a man who never looked down on those who looked up to him, and who helped as many people as he could. As a man who stood up for his beliefs no matter what. As a man who tried to unite all humankind through faith and love. And if all that's too much, then I guess I'd settle for being remembered only as a great boxer who became a leader and a champion of his people. And I wouldn't even mind if folks forgot how pretty I was.

true HAPPINESS

There was a time when I felt the need to show the world how great I was, but I don't have to prove myself anymore. My life's purpose has changed with time and my spirituality has evolved over the years. Everything that I do now, I ask myself, will God be pleased with this? We may think that we have moments alone, but God is there, and always watching.

I conquered the world and it didn't bring me true happiness. The only true happiness comes from honoring God and treating people right.

A SPIRITUAL GOAL

We can never pray enough, or give enough, or share enough, or care about the world enough, and we could never love enough to repay God for his gifts to us.

Being kind to all of his creatures, showing respect for ourselves and others, treating all people with kindness and showing compassion for the less fortunate, ill, and deprived, is what we should do. Knowing this strengthens my faith and turns my faith into spiritual awareness. When we devote all of our actions to a spiritual goal, everything that we do becomes a prayer.

Gratefulness in the character
Is like fragrance in the flower.
—*Sufi Wisdom*

WORKING FOR GOD

I know that I have lived a blessed life. I have nine beautiful children and six grandchildren. I have a loving wife and a beautiful home surrounded by peace and nature. God has been good to me, and I wouldn't change anything that has happened to me. I have learned something from it all. I'm not as physically healthy as I once was, but in many ways I'm a lot stronger now. In order to be truly spiritual, we have to cast aside our material desires and our physical image of ourselves.

A Hindu poet once said, "If the angels who are entirely spiritual could fulfill the purpose of creation, God would have not created man."

I have learned that it is through tragedies that we grow. The losses that we experience, the illnesses that we face, and the pain and sorrow we sometimes feel enable us to achieve our highest and greatest purpose in life, which is spiritual growth.

My greatest accomplishments in life were achieved outside the ring, and my greatest privilege in life was becoming a messenger of peace and love. Because there is nothing as great as working for God.

POSTSCRIPT

the road
TO HEAVEN

A few weeks ago my dad and I were at his house watching old Elvis Presley movies together. Dad is a big fan of Elvis, and in the middle of the movie, Dad reminded me that Elvis had given him a white jeweled robe back in the mid-seventies. It was Saturday afternoon and Lonnie was at one of Asaad's ball games, so it was just the two of us spending the afternoon together. After the movie ended, my dad asked me to drive him to the bookstore in Benton Harbor so he could buy some Bibles and Qurans for a project that he has been working on.

As we were driving down the highway we noticed an elderly black man standing on the corner of the street with a Bible in his hand. We also noticed that he had his thumb up, so we turned around and picked him up. When the man got into the car he told us his name. We will call him Ernie for privacy reasons.

Ernie told us that he just got out of church and asked if we could drop him off a few miles up the road, then he said he would be able to take a cab the rest of the way home. I told Ernie that we would not mind driving him home, but he said he did not want to take us out of our way.

At this point Ernie still had not realized who my father was. When we came to a stop light my dad turned around so that Ernie could see his face. Then Dad said, "We are on our way to the bookstore to buy some Bibles and Qurans, so it won't be out of our way."

Now Ernie recognized my father and said, "Muhammad Ali, well isn't that something!" He went on to say, "Thank you so much for this ride. When we get to my house I have three Bibles I can give you for free."

My father replied, "Thank you, but we'll pay you for them." But Ernie said that he wanted to give them to him to repay him for the ride. My dad asked him what he did for a living.

Ernie told us that he had recently suffered a stroke and that he had had to retire from his job of more than twenty years. My dad then asked Ernie how much money he had in his pocket; Ernie told him about ten dollars.

My father looked at me with wide eyes, leaned over and whispered, "How much money do you have in your purse?" I told him that I would have to go to an ATM to get some cash. Dad asked me to take out as much as I could, so I did. When I got back into the car Ernie and my dad were talking and laughing together like old friends. I handed the money to my father and he turned to Ernie and extended his hand with the money in it.

Ernie looked at the money and asked, "What's this for?"

My dad told him, "It's for you."

Ernie shook his head and exclaimed, "No, no, no, there won't be any of that going on here!"

My dad insisted, "Take the money; I want you to have it! It's for the Bibles that you're going to give me."

But Ernie still would not take it. He said that it was way too much money for three Bibles and that he wanted to give them to Dad, not sell them to him.

Then my dad said, "Take the money. I want to help you." Still Ernie said no.

Dad didn't know what else to do, so he tossed the money into the back seat next to Ernie and said, "You have to take it now!"

Ernie gathered up the cash and said with the most gentle voice, "Mr. Ali, I know that you are very famous and influential, but you can't make a person do something if they don't want to. Even though your intentions are good, I still don't want to take the money." I could see that my father was impressed, but at the same time a little confused. He was so used to people asking him for money before he even had a chance to offer it to them. He seemed at a loss for words.

Then, finally, looking at Ernie with pleading eyes he said, "Take the money, man, I'm trying to get into heaven!"

Responding just as forcefully Ernie told him,

"So am I!"

My father, not taking no for an answer, said one more time, "If you don't take the money, I might not get in!"

To which Ernie replied one last time, "If I do take your money, I might not get in!"

When we reached Ernie's house he introduced us to his wife, of more than thirty years. They have no children and they live in a small, nice home amid a stand of trees. As we were leaving I noticed that my dad had hidden the money under a napkin in the kitchen. I gave Ernie and his wife my phone numbers and told him to call me when he needed a ride to church or anywhere else.

Then as we were getting into the car, Ernie walked over to us, asked us to join hands and said a prayer. As we were driving back home, Dad asked me if I would really go and pick up Ernie if he needed a ride to church. I told him I would. Then he asked, "You would go out of your way to pick him up and then take him all the way home?" Again I said I would, if he needed me to. I noticed my dad's head was down and I could not see his face.

He then looked up at me with tear-filled eyes and said in a soft and gentle voice, "That's me in you." Then he smiled at me and added, "You're on the road to heaven."

—Hana Yasmeen Ali

THE SOUL OF A BUTTERFLY

It was not my father's heavyweight championships that made him great; it was not his Olympic success, or his victory over the government. His greatness lies in his ability to keep love in his heart through all of the upheavals of life. His greatness is in his courage, it's in his strength, and it's in his compassion. In my eyes, he was even greater at being a loving father than he was at being a world champion.

He was great in the way that he made sure all of his children knew and respected each other. He taught us life's most valuable lessons, not just with his words and moral opinions, but through his actions. He taught us about kindness, about friendship, about compassion, about generosity, about virtue, and about love. His office door was never closed, not even when he had important interviews and work to do. He was there for us even when he was away. He showered us all with affection and love, and made each of us feel special. He told me bedtime stories until I fell asleep at night. He brought my lunch to school. He helped me eat my vegetables, so I could have dessert. He always stood by me, no matter what. And he recorded every word that we had to say. He was great in his singular way of making me feel important.

With all of the prizes, trophies, awards, and treasures that my father has received and given away, his greatness lay in the way he kept the recordings of his children's voices protected in a small safe.

Dad, believe me when I say that in my eyes you are the world's greatest father, not because you were perfect, but because you gave us the greatest gift any parent could ever give a child . . . Yourself. You no longer have to communicate with words; your eyes express what is in your heart and your smile tells the story of love.

Whatever the future holds for my father, know that this is true . . . He has lived a life dedicated to God, and all that devotion lives on inside him. He has lived his life with strength and courage, and those virtues live on inside him. He has lived a life in pursuit of peace, now all that peace resides inside him. And he's lived a life full of love, and all of that love lives on inside him.

He is happy, he is at peace, and he truly loves being Muhammad Ali.

—Hana Yasmeen Ali

THE SOUL OF A
BUTTERFLY

WITHIN THE HANDS OF TIME

He no longer has the energy to walk against the wind,

So he has decided to make time a friend.

There are no limits while turning the hands of time,

All past and present moments are forever entwined.

Somewhere in the distance are shadows of the butterfly,

where all that once flourished, carries on in his mind.

Where youth and health will always thrive,

Where strength and speed are eternally fine,

And Golden Gloves still shine.

For all that he has gained and lost in sight of a greater good,

he weathered the storm with elegance and style,

beside a grace wherein truth stood

Now as the years pass, as age overtakes and grows.

There will be more stories told of legendary goals.

In retrospect of yesterday, remember what was great.

True heroes are those with hearts of gold,

and ideals that never fade.

So when you seek to know this glory, look to the open sky,

Where all that he has loved is treasured,

Always and forever prime, within the *Soul of a Butterfly*.

—Hana Yasmeen Ali

acknowledgments

First and foremost, I want to praise God for providing all of the spiritual advisers and teachers who have taught me and guided me throughout my life. Without them, this book would not have been possible. Even the simple discovery of a great book is a blessing.

I'd like to give a special thanks to my family—my wife, Lonnie, and all of my beautiful children—for their unconditional love.

Muhammad and Hana would like to thank the following people for helping make this book possible.

Susan Crawford, Hana's literary agent for this book, for all her countless labors and endless hours that she has contributed, along with her support and enthusiasm. Bob Bender, our editor at Simon & Schuster, for his dedication and patience. Ron DiNicola, who is a good lawyer and a family friend. Special thanks to my brother, Rahaman, and to my old friend Gene Kilroy for sharing their wonderful memories, Howard Bingham for contributing his timeless photos, and last but certainly not least, Deborah Seager and David Chaudoir for their invaluable assistance. And a special thank you to Tom Hauser for his cooperation and generosity. We are grateful to all of you. You were each essential in making this book what it is.

*   *   *

Hana also wishes to bestow a very special thank you on her mother, Veronica Porche Anderson: Thank you, Mother, for strengthening my confidence in myself, encouraging me to do my best, and believing in me like no one else. I love you dearly.

the muhammad ali center

The Muhammad Ali Center will open in the fall of 2005 in Ali's hometown of Louisville, Kentucky. It will be an international cultural and educational center that is dedicated to the ideals Muhammad has exemplified throughout his life. Like Muhammad himself, the Ali Center will focus on what brings people together, not what sets them apart.

Visitor experiences at the Muhammad Ali Center focus on six defining themes of Ali's legacy: Respect, Confidence, Conviction, Dedication, Giving, and Spirituality. These themes are explored through remarkable interactive and multimedia learning experiences and exploratory galleries. Visitors follow the story of Ali's journey and are invited to embark on their own paths to personal success. Through extensive educational outreach, international partnerships, exhibits and distance-learning programming, the Center will reach individuals across the country and around the world.

www.alicenter.org